I've Got a Feelin' Everything's Gonna Be All Right

I've Got a Feelin'
Everything's Gonna Be All Right

.

I've Got a Feelin'
Everything's Gonna Be All Right
ISBN 0-89274-911-3
Copyright © 1992 by Carlton Pearson
P.O. Box 700007
Tulsa, Oklahoma 74170

Published by Harrison House, Inc.
P.O. Box 35035
Tulsa, Oklahoma 74153

I've Got a Feelin'
Everything's Gonna Be All Right

by
Carlton Pearson

Harrison House
Tulsa, Oklahoma

Contents

Preface

I would like to share with you a portion of my personal testimony in order to set the stage for the message which I believe the Lord has laid on my heart to deliver to His Church in these pages. My purpose is not to glorify myself but to emphasize the call to personal righteousness and true holiness which I believe the Lord is issuing to all His people as we face the crucial, challenging days which lie ahead.

Back in the early 1950s, there was a young married couple in San Diego, California, who had had three children. Both of these young people had been raised in the Holiness movement in the Church of God in Christ.

Over the years they had backslidden but recommitted their lives to Christ when the wife became pregnant with their fourth child. While the young woman was in her fourth pregnancy, she attended a revival. During that series of meetings, the evangelist asked the people to go on a three-day and -night fast. This is not done much in our churches any more. When the fast was called, the young woman was a bit concerned because she was not sure whether, in her condition, she should attempt to fast.

But the Lord led her to consult with some of the older ladies in the church who assured her that it would be perfectly safe for her to take part in the fast if she felt so spiritually inclined. During the three days, she fasted and prayed. At the end of the period of fasting, the evangelist called this young woman to the front of the church and prayed over her womb, prophesying over the unborn baby. He told her that her baby would be mightily used of God.

A few months later, she went to the hospital and gave birth to a nine-pound, eight-ounce boy. The woman was my mother. She named me Carlton Dmetrius Pearson.

The hand of God was upon me from the beginning. One of my earliest remembrances is being left with some ladies in a church meeting, at the tender age of eighteen months, while my mother worked in the church kitchen.

Because I cried so much, my mother finally came to comfort me, softly explaining that I should not cry because "Mother is working for the Lord." That statement gripped my heart, and I began to feel the presence of the Lord in my young life.

At about the age of four and a half, I was sitting under a piano bench in my home looking through a book called *Portrait of Jesus*. I noticed all the pictures of Jesus blessing the children, healing the blind, and raising the dead. Then I came to the picture depicting the crucifixion. I could not understand why this man who had been so good and kind to everyone should have to be suffering such torment and agony. Tears began to stream down my face. It was as if the Holy Spirit had taken me into the picture so I could stand at the foot of the cross and look up at Jesus as He hung there. I began to feel the hurt and the compassion that Jesus felt, and I wept.

My mother was talking on the phone when she noticed that I was crying.

"What's wrong, son?" she asked.

And all I could do was hold up to her the little book. Immediately she hung up the receiver, sat me up on the dining room table and told me the story of Jesus. She did not ask me that night if I would like to accept Jesus as my Savior and Lord, but at that early age, I made a conscious decision in my heart that I was going to serve the man in that book for the rest of my life.

All through grade school, junior high school and high school, the hand of God remained upon me. I had already been preaching mock sermons since childhood, sometimes using an inverted trash can set up in the back yard as a makeshift pulpit. When I was in high school, I began to feel the Lord calling me to go on to college, something none of my family had ever done. Because I felt led to reach for something bigger and better for my life, I went to my father and told him, "I want to go to Oral Roberts University."

"Son, I'm not financially able to send you to college," my father answered sorrowfully.

"Dad," I replied, "you may not be able to send me, but my heavenly Father is going to provide me the way to go."

The family began to pray. My mother and I went on a seven-day fast. At the end of the seven days, a man called and said, "Son, I understand you want to go to college."

"Yes sir, I do," I responded.

"Well, I'm going to send you, and give you a hundred dollars a month for expenses."

God miraculously provided, just as had been prophesied.

In the fall of 1971, I arrived in Tulsa, Oklahoma. Within two weeks of my arrival, I was approached by President Roberts himself who asked me, "Son, do you sing?"

"Yes sir, I try," I answered.

"Well, I want you to meet my son, Richard."

The following spring I became a member of the Oral Roberts University World Action Singers — and the rest of my schooling was paid for. From this experience, I learned how true it is that where God guides, He provides.

In 1971, while walking through the prayer gardens at ORU, I met a young man named Gary McIntosh. Instantly a spiritual union was forged between us by the Lord. We became fast friends and began to share with each other our most cherished dreams and visions. Now, over twenty years later, we are still being used together of the Lord in the ministry.

I was at ORU for five and a half years, and then I was asked to accept the position as associate evangelist for the Oral Roberts Evangelistic Association. The position had only been held previously by one man, Bob Deweese, who had resigned after years of faithful service to open a church in Florida.

I began to help answer the mail which came to the evangelistic association and to minister to the ladies who responded to the people who wrote in describing their desperate situations and needs. Although I was afforded the very best treatment and enjoyed the most wonderful services and opportunities imaginable, I felt that I was not fulfilling my God-ordained calling. I had an itching and burning in my heart. I knew it was the spirit of personal evangelism. I was convinced that God wanted me to go out and share the Good News with other people.

So in 1977, I began to fast and pray, seeking God's guidance and direction. As I did so, I felt the Lord leading me to resign my position as associate evangelist and to launch my own ministry. When I told my mother that I believed it was the Lord's will for me to "step down" from my position and go into full-time evangelism, she replied, "Son, if that is what the Lord has told you to do, you're not stepping down, you're stepping up."

Based on that statement, the Holy Spirit quickened to my spirit Isaiah 55:8,9: "...my thoughts are not your thoughts, neither are your ways my ways," declares the Lord. "As the heavens are higher than the earth, so are my ways higher than your ways and my thoughts than your thoughts." From that word came the title Higher Dimensions, the name of the ministry which I launched that same year, 1977. It is still in existence today.

I assembled a ministry team, and we began to travel the country. God opened many doors, but there were also trying times. Six months into the ministry, every road team member quit except one. But as I continued to release my heart and spirit to God, the Lord's will began to prevail.

From 1977 to 1981, I traveled widely, ministering to thousands of people. However, I began to realize that in the 1980s the Lord was going to start doing a new work. No longer was God going to work only through so-called superstar evangelists. Now He was going to work through His Body, the Church.

I knew that I could not go out as one man alone and reach the entire world for Jesus. But I saw that I could plant my vision in the hearts of others who would become evangelists, carrying the Gospel around the world. So I started a church by the same name — Higher Dimensions. Gary McIntosh joined me in this new work for the Lord.

After months of searching for a suitable building and location where people of all races, ages and social, economic and intellectual levels would feel comfortable and welcome, Gary and I rented a place in Jenks, a suburb on the southern edge of Tulsa, Oklahoma. The first service was held on August 31, 1981. There were approximately seventy-five people in attendance. Within three weeks, the church was trying to figure out how to tear out the walls to make more room. God blessed us so richly that we had to begin holding two services instead of one.

Soon attendance was up to five hundred to six hundred people. There was just no more room. Through a series of miraculous events, the Lord provided a much larger, more modern and better-equipped building in the fastest-growing residential and commercial area of town. The Lord had a reason for placing Higher Dimensions Evangelistic Center in that ideal location. Since the time of its establishment, it has continued to grow and expand, meeting the needs of thousands of people.

It is exciting now to look back over the past and see the way the Lord has blessed this church with its excellent facilities, magnificent choir, glorious musicians and wonderful congregation. But it did not all happen instantaneously or effortlessly. As in any endeavor for the Lord, there were challenges to meet and obstacles to overcome.

One problem was a lack of funds. Another was a lack of available qualified personnel. I had to keep traveling constantly, leaving Gary to carry on the work of the church by himself. Sometimes the congregation would be without a musician to lead worship services, so my mother would have to play. At other times there wouldn't be anyone to provide musical accompaniment. There were about twenty people in the choir and many of them didn't know how to sing. There was seldom enough money to buy needed supplies and pay salaries. The church just had to get along the best way it could with the limited financial and human resources available to it. But God blessed and anointed the work.

People kept telling Gary and me that we would never succeed. People said that one of our troubles was that we were trying to attract both blacks and whites to the same church. We were told that it was impossible to have a multi-racial congregation, that blacks and whites and Hispanics and Indians could not worship together in harmony. At first there were some struggles. But the team persevered, and God began to bless our efforts.

Then one night the Lord gave me a revelation. He showed me that Higher Dimensions is not a melting pot, that it is not its purpose to change whites into blacks or blacks into whites.

We are not a melting pot, we are a stew. In a melting pot everything is reduced to one indiscriminate mass. But in a stew each ingredient retains its own unique nature and identity. Each lends its distinctive flavor to the whole.

In our church all of us of different races, cultures and backgrounds learn to accept, love and appreciate one another. We don't expect anyone to change and become what we are. The Lord is maturing us as we grow. He has been good to us, and we are excited as we celebrate our tenth anniversary.

We like to say that ours is a church in which everyone is an evangelist. We don't emphasize ordination credentials. We accept individually Christ's commission to go into the world and preach and teach, heal the sick and raise the dead. God has given us the ability and power, as members of the Body of Christ, to do the same works that Christ Himself did. We believe that He has done the same for every body of believers everywhere in the world. The problem is that we in the Church have not taken that power and authority and acted upon it. But now God is calling all of us to be evangelists and to go forth and produce much fruit for His Kingdom.

That does not mean going to our job with our Bible under our arm, laying hands on someone's head and spewing forth tongues. Rather it is showing forth Jesus in our daily lives.

People are tired of the talk. They want to see the walk.

The same is true in the Body of Christ. Most people would rather see a sermon than hear one any day. I don't want to say that I know and serve Jesus, and then treat people as though I have never heard of the Lord. God is requiring us to take on His character, His nature, and His likeness. People want to see Jesus. They are sick and tried of religious junk, of false super piety. Much of what has been going on in Christian circles is a stench in the nostrils of God. And it has become a stench in our nostrils also. Many of the very men who once commanded great crowds did not have command over their own personal lives. That situation has got to change, and I believe the change has already begun.

Many people have power with God. Elijah did. God called him, set him apart and sent him to the mission field. He was miraculously fed by ravens and by a poor widow, to whose dead son he imparted life. Then he went up on Mount Carmel where he overcame 850 prophets of Baal and Asherah by calling down fire from heaven. (1 Kings 18:19,40.)

Elijah did many great things. But then, right after demonstrating his enormous power with men and with God, Elijah turned coward, fleeing from a woman named Jezebel who had made threats against his life. Although filled with the power of the Spirit, he ran from the works of the flesh.

In this day God is requiring us to have power over ourselves, strength of character. Without it, the glory of God cannot be revealed as it needs to be in the Church. The reason it is so difficult for us to win to the Lord the people we live with, work with and interact with on a daily basis is because they know us too well.

Our spouses, our children, our friends and coworkers know us intimately. They see behind the facade we present to the general public. They know what we are like behind closed doors, in private, when we are alone. It is that secret nature that God is dealing with now — the nature that keeps people from seeing Jesus in us.

How can we demonstrate our worst nature to people around us and then expect them to accept our invitation to come to church with us or to accept our Lord? We must quit living a double standard. We must develop self-control, self-discipline, power over our flesh, so that our walk comes up to our talk. Then perhaps others will become more interested in what we profess to believe.

We can go to church, read the Bible, receive the anointing of God, and spend time on our knees in prayer, but what is most important is what we do once we get up off our knees and go out into the world to interact with others.

God doesn't deal with us only when we are on our knees in prayer. He also deals with us as we go through our daily routine of life. If the Lord reveals to me in prayer that I have a spirit of pride, I can ask Him to remove it from me. But if I then go out and deal pridefully with my coworkers and others, then my prayer has been for naught.

Jesus said, "When you come to the altar to present a gift to the Lord, if you have an unresolved conflict with another person, first go straighten out that situation, then come and offer your gift." We have a tendency to do just the opposite. We come to the altar and ask God to set things right in our life — usually by straightening out the other person! Now, in these days, God is expecting us to set our own affairs in order first, before we come to His altar of grace.

God is calling His people higher. We must learn to walk on a higher plane, in a higher realm, in a higher dimension (as we call our church in Tulsa). We must come to walk in the character and nature of God. That spiritual posture is called holiness.

Holiness is not just following a particular code of dress, makeup and hair styling. It is not just avoiding certain worldly places and pastimes. It is not just related to church attendance, Bible reading, tithing, or other worthwhile and beneficial religious endeavors and disciplines. Holiness is taking on the nature and character of the Lord Jesus Christ.

If we don't do that, all of our prayer, praise and worship is for nothing. We must do as my father has always told me to do: We must be what we are looking for.

What are we in the Church of Jesus Christ looking for? Are we looking for a Church that is washed in the blood of the Lamb, a Church that is without spot or wrinkle? If so, we must remember that spots and wrinkles come out only by having cleansing, heat and pressure applied to them. The Lord is going to allow some cleansing, heat and pressure to be applied to us, His Body, in order to remove the spots and wrinkles in our lives — personally and corporately — so that we can truly become His glorious Church.

The Great Commission states: **Go ye into all the world, and preach the gospel to every creature.** (Mark 16:15 KJV) That word *preach* means ''to herald,'' ''to give forth,'' ''to proclaim.'' How can we proclaim divine truth if we are not walking in truth ourselves? In this new day, we must learn to walk and live in divine truth in order for God's Word and glory to be revealed to the world.

It is not enough for us just to fill our churches with warm bodies who pray and praise and then go out and live the same selfish, acquisitive, ego-centered lives as those about them in the world. Who does that glorify? It is only as we come together in harmony and love, allowing God to do His refining process on us, working the rough edges off of us, that we will begin to affect the world with the Gospel. We must live it before we can give it.

God is tired of our saying yes and living no. It is time for the Church of Jesus Christ to arise and commit to live lives befitting the glorious Name we bear. God is constantly giving us opportunities to minister to people in need. Each of us has an opportunity to minister to someone every day. Maybe it is nothing more than a chance to comfort or encourage another person, to pat him on the back, to say, "God loves you." But most of us are not listening. We don't have our spiritual ears tuned in to the Spirit of the Lord.

The Bible says that some sow and some water, while others reap the harvest. Who knows what will come as the result of our sowing just one seed of love and kindness in the life of another individual? Every day the Lord brings us into contact with other people to whom we can be Jesus. Every day we have a chance, as the telephone commercial says, to "reach out and touch someone." When we touch another life with the love of Christ, it is never for naught. No act of love is ever wasted effort.

The Lord has each person's life charted out. God has defined a course for each individual to follow that will bless him, minister to him, and bring him to a saving knowledge of the Lord Jesus Christ. You and I have been chosen, commissioned and anointed to play a part in the fulfillment of that plan.

I am excited about this coming season of new beginnings in the Church. I believe God is going to start doing something new in the hearts and lives of His people. He is going to start taking us at our word. We can't just sit in the pew any longer and content ourselves with the knowledge that we are the redeemed of the Lord, the righteousness of God in Christ. Now we must rise up as a body and go out into all the world to carry the Gospel of Jesus Christ to every creature.

Evangelism is not preaching. It is not learning and quoting scriptures. It is not arguing against the beliefs and practices of other Christians. Evangelism is spreading the Good News. It is shedding abroad the love and light of Jesus Christ. As we do that, there will never be a building erected large enough to hold us. We won't be proselyting — recruiting members from other churches. We won't be competing or finding fault with other parts of the Body of Christ. People will listen to us and be drawn to make a commitment of their lives to the Lord because we have reached out and touched them — in the grocery store, in the classroom, on the playing field and in the office. That's what God wants us, His people, to do — win the world with love.

That's what Jesus did. He went out into the streets and ministered to the people where they were, where they lived, where they hurt. We are to become actively involved in a local body of believers, but we must not become arrogant and complacent. We must not become self-satisfied, self-centered, self-important. We must not become so wrapped up in feeding ourselves and our own spiritual hunger that we fail to go out into the highways and hedges and compel others to come in and feed at the Master's table. We must never allow soul-stirring sermons to replace soulwinning service.

May we never become stagnant. May we be a fountain of life, a river of refreshing water, flowing out to reach others with the love and light of the Lord.

May each of us commit ourselves to become an evangelist, dedicated to carrying to the world the glorious Gospel of peace — the Good News of Jesus Christ.

That has been the calling, purpose and thrust of my entire life. Won't you join me as we reach out to others and draw them with cords of love?

Carlton Pearson

Introduction

With the world economy, particularly the United States economy, tottering on the brink of destruction and annihilation, with a recession already in progress and with a threat of a depression if things continue as they are, the Church must have some clear responses and answers to the questions and problems of the day.

God wants to speak directly through the Church because in times of crisis, God raises His head and shines on the Church, showing the world as a beacon light how to get out of its despair and misery. We must be God's people with a new completion, a new maximization of the call. As Brother Turnell Nelson, a pastor in Trinidad, has said, God did not save us just for heaven. I believe God created us and we were born for fellowship with Him, but we were saved for warfare. And in the warfare, we become a light and testimony to a doubting and hostile world. It is becoming clearer to me with age and experience who we are as believers and what our purpose is.

Our purpose is to overcome abuse.

Abuse occurs when we don't understand our purpose.[1] If we did not understand the purpose of a microphone or lectern or sound system or musical instruments, we would abuse them. A person who doesn't know the purpose of his spouse or children tends to abuse them. If you don't know the purpose of the chemicals that come out of the earth, you abuse them and they become harmful drugs. The Church is abused, and abuses itself. We abuse the gifts of God and the teachings on prosperity and healing and the blessing of God for the Church because we don't understand their purpose.

---

[1]Myles Monroe, *Understanding Your Potential* (Skippensburg: Destiny Image, 1991).

The purpose isn't just to make us individually happy, though that's part of it. The main purpose of prosperity is to rub the devil's nose in the victory of the Church and to let the unbelieving world know that our God is the great God. In this book, I would like to share with you on the subject of biblical prosperity, but I don't want to use that term, because it is overused and misinterpreted. Rather I would like to emphasize the difference between blessings and cursings.

Both are from God. They are found in the book of Deuteronomy. The word *deuteronomy* means "second law giving." It means to remember or repeat or rehearse or rehash the things God had said forty years earlier when Moses brought the children of Israel out of Egypt. When they arrived at Mount Sinai, they received the Law, the Ten Commandments. Moses made commentary on these laws in his 120th year as he stood looking at the other side of the Jordan, which he would not enter in the natural, because he would soon depart and go into the presence of God.

Moses' days were numbered, his time had expired. He was going to be taken from the children of Israel, and he knew it. So he was about to speak to a whole different generation from the one he had led out of bondage. Forty years had passed and this was a young generation who did not remember the Red Sea, the manna from heaven, the water that came out of the rock. They did not know the power that was in the rod that Moses used or that Moses' shoes never wore out and his clothes never frayed. That generation did not know what it was to stand in fear and yet in awe of God. Their fathers and mothers had received the blessings of the Lord and experienced them, and now they were gone.

I'm very happy I was born in 1953 in one of the most peaceful decades in this century. It was right after WWII in which my father fought. I'm a post-WWII child. I'm of that baby-boom generation. I remember mothers hanging clothes on the clothesline, and they never had to worry about them being stolen. I remember eating Cheerios and Wheat Chex and Shredded Wheat and Rice Krispies and maybe a few others. Today we have rows and rows of cold cereal. There are so many to choose from you don't know what to buy.

I remember watching ABC and NBC and CBS with "I Love Lucy" and "Popeye, the Sailor Man" and "Father Knows Best" and "My Three Sons." Very nice, warm, nostalgic-type programs. They didn't have as many guns and wars in those days as we do now. Now we've got sixty stations to look at. In those days we had three, and that was black and white and we had to have our antenna just right or we could get only one of them. The way we fixed the TV in that day was to hit it. We didn't have automatic garage openers, and no one had wrought iron on his windows and doors to keep out the thieves. We kept the doors open and unlocked, and everybody shared together.

I remember the days when you went to buy shampoo, you bought it and used it to wash your hair. But today you don't know whether to wash your hair with the stuff or eat it. You've got dreamy, creamy, pistachio, peanut butter. Every kind of flavor for just shampoo. We're living in a day of too many choices and too little time, so people are confused.

I remember as a little boy standing and saying the pledge of allegiance with such pride in my heart. I remember singing the Star Spangled Banner and sometimes even saluting. I remember all of us stopping while the principal of the school gave a corporate prayer over the loudspeaker system and we'd all bow our heads. Some of the teachers even read a scripture. I remember the days when God opened the Red Seas for America and poured out blessings on her. It was in that decade that we added the words, "under God," to the pledge of allegiance, in 1954. And in 1956 ratified as our national model legal statement of faith, "in God we trust." That all happened in the decade of the '50s when the Billy Grahams and the Oral Roberts were young men, just getting started, full of the Holy Ghost and blazing a sawdust trail all across the country.

Now those days have gone.

As school kids, we used to get in trouble for shooting paper wads or chewing gum. Now youngsters get in trouble for killing one another, for raping other students in the bathroom, for stabbing school teachers. How we have declined over the years. The great leaders of 30 or 40 years ago are now in their final days. They're like Moses; they're looking at the other side. They're going on to their reward and we're asking, where are the next leaders? Where is the new anointing? Where is the fresh flow of the Holy Spirit? Who's going to take us on now?

Can we recoup what we've lost? Can we recover what we've forfeited as a nation? I know that we can, but I'm really not sure that we will. We're not casting out devils. We're not taking the communities back. We're not exercising our rights and authority as believers.

I'm declaring war on the devil. I want him to know that I'm here and that, in the name of Jesus, we're going to take back what has been stolen from us. Do you believe we have the anointing to break the curse that's on the American society? We do. And we must exercise our power as the people of God.

"The quality of a man's life will be in direct proportion to his commitment to excellence." That's what former head coach of the Dallas Cowboys, Tom Landry, said. The meaning of one's life will be determined by the power that controls it. What power or influence governs your life?

I believe in excellence. I believe in the Church, in Jesus Christ. I'm proud of what we stand for and who we are. I haven't the slightest notion of abdicating. It is time for the Church to rise like an island in the sea of crisis and point the way to Jesus.

Hear, O Israel

In his final address to the children of Israel, Moses said,

Hear now, O Israel, the decrees and laws I am about to teach you. Follow them so that you may live and may go in and take possession of the land that the Lord, the God of your fathers, is giving you.

Deuteronomy 4:1

I want you to see this promised land as not only geographical soil. I want you to see it as a new generation of men and women God is raising up to go into the decade of the '90s and the twenty-first century to seize the land for God — to bring restoration, reformation, and revival.

Keep the Lord's Commands

We're coming into a different era of time. Moses told the people of his day,

Do not add to what I command you and do not subtract from it, but keep the commands of the Lord your God that I give you.

Deuteronomy 4:2

That is my message to the Church of Jesus Christ today, the message I want to share in these pages.

The Lord Is Near Us

What other nation [what other people, what other country] **is so great as to have their gods near them the way the Lord our God is near us whenever we pray to him?**

Deuteronomy 4:7

The other nations had polytheism, many gods. But like Israel, we have one God, the Lord Jehovah. What other people, what other church besides the Christian Church, what other nation, is so blessed as we? At this time it was Israel, now I really believe it's America.

We have been the nation that has evangelized the world. I know that sounds arrogant and proud. I'm not saying that America is the only special nation in the world. America is losing her place. She was at one time the number one lender nation, now she has become the number one debtor nation.

Inheritance of Righteousness

And what other nation is so great as to have such righteous decrees and laws as this body of laws I am setting before you today?
Deuteronomy 4:8

What other nation is so great as to have such righteous decrees as the Declaration of Independence, the Constitution, the Preamble, and the Bible?

Be Careful Not To Forget

Only be careful, and watch yourselves closely so that you do not forget the things your eyes have seen or let them slip from your heart as long as you live.
Deuteronomy 4:9

I will not forget the peace that I grew up under. I will not forget the peace I had in my little neighborhood. I will not forget the patriotism and godliness of our society then. I will not forget the anointing I felt in those little churches that weren't nearly as large as these mega-churches we have today, churches in which everybody loved one another and shared together freely. I'm glad I came along at the end of that generation so I can take some of that spirit with me on into the next century.

Remember the Days Gone By

Remember the day you stood before the Lord your God at Horeb, when he said to me, "Assemble the people before me to hear my words so that they may learn to revere [or reverence or fear] me as long as they live in the land and may teach them to their children."
Deuteronomy 4:10

Back when Billy Graham and Oral Roberts were young, the nation would listen to them very profoundly, much more so than now because our generation doesn't remember their great influence. The younger generation doesn't remember the great tent revivals. They don't remember the packed-out stadiums. They don't remember the spiritual excitement and the hunger for God of those days. All they remember is the latest rock star, the latest movie. All they remember is PacMan eating away all their frustration. You go to those video arcades, and there's nothing in there but violence.

We're comfortable with violence in our society today because it comes into our homes by television all the time. If you stop some time on Saturday and watch the cartoons, notice all the supernatural influences, but there's never reference to Jesus, never anything referring to the Bible. We don't see anything about God unless He's represented in a negative context.

America wasn't like that when I was young. There was a day when the wheels of commerce ceased on Sunday morning. The stores shut down on Sunday and people went to church and served God. Families sat down and ate together. We've got to get back to that day when we respected the sanctity of the home.

America is under siege. It is under a curse. But if you read what the Word of God says, you will see that we, as God's people, are blessed.

The Lord Our God Is One

Hear, O Israel: The Lord our God, the Lord is one.
Deuteronomy 6:4

Hear, O America, hear O Christian Church, the Lord our God, the Lord is one.

Love the Lord Wholeheartedly

Love the Lord your God with all your heart and with all your soul and with all your strength.
Deuteronomy 6:5

Let Him be the center of your life. In Hebrew, to *love* means "to have affection, sexually or otherwise, to romance, and to have love as for a friend." It's a word that means "to have desire for."

Keep God's Word in Your Heart

These commandments that I give you today are to be upon your hearts. Impress them on your children. Talk about them when you sit at home and when you walk along the road, when you lie down and when you get up. Tie them as symbols on your hands and bind them on your foreheads. Write them on the doorframes of your houses and on your gates.

Deuteronomy 6:6-9

Let's get back to the family altars in our homes.

Why don't you take my advice and take at least one night a week for reading. Shut down the TV and VCR. At least for a few hours, sit together in the living room and read. Some of my most precious memories are when my family sat down together. My mother would take the books and read them to us. Many times she and Daddy would read to each other. She would be reading a story and I often sat and listened.

Read. Then have a family altar and talk about the things of God. That is one important step toward preserving our families, toward redeeming America for the Lord, toward reviving and restoring the Church of Jesus Christ.

To accomplish the task which lies before us in the days ahead, we must become a Church endued with the power and presence of the Lord — a Church with a double portion of God's anointing.

1

The Blessing of Obedience

> If you fully obey the Lord your God and carefully
> follow all his commands I give you today, the Lord
> your God will set you high above all the nations on
> earth. All these blessings will come upon you and
> accompany you if you obey the Lord your God.
>
> However, if you do not obey the Lord your God
> and do not carefully follow all his commands and
> decrees I am giving you today, all these curses will
> come upon you and overtake you.
>
> **Deuteronomy 28:1,2,15**

We have perverted the message of prosperity and
taught it sensually only. The word *sensual* has to do with
the senses: sight, hearing, tasting, smelling, touching. But
I want to take the sensation out of prosperity and make it
a spiritual appropriation in your life.

I want you to understand by the Spirit what these
blessings are, and the curses, too, for they will affect your
senses and the things that appeal to your base nature. But
your heart, your spirit, your emotions have to be that which
grasp the truth. I want to take Old Testament legalism and
spiritualize it and make it liberation.

The reason the children of Israel had to have the law
in their hands was because they did not have it in their
hearts. In the Old Testament the Lord says (and Paul speaks
of it in Corinthians) that He will take the law out of tablets
of stone and put it in tablets of human hearts.

Tablets of human hearts. You and I can get this "law"
in our spirit. The whole world is waiting to hear a people
of God who know the Lord personally.

A People Blessed of God

The Lord your God will set you high above all the
nations on earth. (Deut. 28:1.) In this passage the Hebrew
word translated *nations* is *ethnos* in Greek, from which we

27

get the English word *ethnic*. The Lord is not just talking about Jews and Arabs and Mexicans and other nationalities. He is talking about a spiritual nation. A holy nation.

When I travel abroad, people want to know what nationality I am. When I first thought about it, I had to say American Negro. Then in the '60s I was told I was Black so I said American Negro and Black. Then I began to study the Scriptures, particularly in Peter's epistle where he says that we are a chosen generation, a royal priesthood, a holy nation. Now I have to say American Negro Black and Holy.

Obedience Produces Blessing

All these blessings will come upon you and accompany you if you *obey* the Lord your God. (Deut. 28:2.) The *King James Version* says if you "hearken" ("diligently" — v. 1). The word *hearken* starts in English with the word hear. If you *hear*. That really means to hear intelligently. Hear kinetically. The word *kinetic* means "in motion."

There is potential energy, and there is kinetic energy. Potential energy is the energy in the piano when it's not being played. It's just potential, dormant energy. But kinetic energy is energy that is in motion, energy that is put into practice.

The Bible tells us that faith without works is dead or dormant. (James 2:17.) Faith without works is potential. Faith with works is kinetic faith. That is action, and it brings deliverance.

So Moses says, "If you hearken. If you hear intelligently. If you accept and receive. If you hear recognizably. If you can understand what you're hearing in your spirit and appropriate it in your life. If you obey fully, and carefully, tediously, reverently, obediently, follow all the Lord's appointments to you, all His commands which I give you today, then the Lord your God will set you high above all nations on the earth."

That does not just apply to Israel.

It did at that time. God was using Israel as a sign. But it really applies to all believers. In Galatians, the Apostle Paul tells us that all who believe and are baptized in Christ are sons of Abraham. Heirs of the promise. But not all who come from Abraham are Israel. Not all of those who are biological children of Abraham are spiritual Israel. Paul made that statement himself, and he was a Jew.

We Christians today in many senses are modern New Testament Israel, full of the Holy Ghost. Remember, Jesus was a Jew. He was the Christ or Messiah. But we Christians are a part, in the Spirit, of the whole Jewish culture.

Set on High

He will set you on high. (Deut. 28:1.) This word translated *high* is *elyown* in Hebrew. It comes from a root word meaning "to mount, ascend, or elevate." God is saying, "I will elevate you. I will ascend you. I will classify you or rank you higher, even than your enemies." God says that we will become classified people.

I am bought with a price. I am full of the Holy Ghost. I am God's private property. I'm not saying that in arrogance, I'm saying that defensively. I want the devil to know that I know who I am. I know my purpose. And my position. God has classified me above all nations.

All These Blessings

All these blessings will come on you. (Deut. 28:2.) In Hebrew, that word *blessings* means "benedictions." All these benedictions, all these prosperities, all these liberalities, all this generosity will come upon you and "overtake" you, says the *King James Version*. The *New International Bible* says they will "accompany you." How would you like to be overtaken with blessings, continually accompanied by blessings?

The Lord has promised that all these blessings will come upon us and overtake us. And accompany us. If we obey.

I will obey the Lord. I will hear the Word and I will respond. That's more than just submitting to God. It's really devotion and reverence based on the reception of knowledge.

The Blessing of the Lord

You will be blessed in the city and blessed in the country.

The fruit of your womb will be blessed, and the crops of your land and the young of your livestock — the calves of your herds and the lambs of your flocks.

Your basket and your kneading trough will be blessed.

You will be blessed when you come in and blessed when you go out.

The Lord will grant that the enemies who rise up against you will be defeated before you. They will come at you from one direction but flee from you in seven.

The Lord will send a blessing on your barns and on everything you put your hand to. The Lord your God will bless you in the land he is giving you.

The Lord will establish you as his holy people, as he promised you on oath, if you keep the commands of the Lord your God and walk in his ways. Then all the peoples on earth will see that you are called by the name of the Lord, and they will fear you. The Lord will grant you abundant prosperity — in the fruit of your womb, the young of your livestock and the crops of your ground — in the land he swore to your forefathers to give you.

The Lord will open the heavens, the storehouse of his bounty, to send rain on your land in season and to bless all the work of your hands. You will lend to many nations but will borrow from none. The Lord will make you the head, not the tail. If you pay attention to the commands of the Lord your God that I give you this day and carefully follow them, you will always be at the top, never at the bottom. Do not turn aside from any of the commands I give you today, to

the right or to the left, following after other gods and serving them.

Deuteronomy 28:3-14

You are devoted to God. You revere Him. You worship Him. Because you know Him, because you recognize Him to be God, you will be blessed, prosperous, liberal. You will receive generously in the inner-cities or urban areas, and you'll be blessed and prosperous in the country — the suburbs and rural areas. The fruit of your womb will be blessed. That means your children will be blessed.

And the crops of your land will prosper. Israel was a rural society. They had livestock and crops. Today the Lord would say, ''You'll be blessed on your job, in your source or means of income.''

Your basket and your trough — that which you make and sell with your hands — will be blessed.

The Lord will grant that the enemies who rise up against you will be defeated before you. Remember Proverbs 16:7 says that if a man's ways are pleasing to the Lord, He will make his enemies live at peace with him. Your enemies will come against you, but they'll also flee. They'll come from one direction and flee from you in seven. The use of the word *seven* indicates there will be a complete destruction for your adversaries.

The Lord will send a blessing on your barns and on everything you put your hand to. The Lord your God will bless you in the land He is giving you. The Lord will establish you with His holy people as He promised you on oath if you keep the commands of the Lord your God and walk in His ways. The word *keep* means ''to guard or protect.'' And to *walk* means literally ''to carry, to make a path.''

All peoples on earth will see that you are called or known or famous (the word actually means ''published, recognized, identified, or surnamed'') by the name of the Lord. Everybody will know that your last name is of God. (v. 10.)

31

They refer to us as the Pearson family or the McIntosh family or the McClendon family. So whatever the blessing is on the head of the family, that is a blessing that should be on the children. When the Lord says that you'll be called by His name, He means that your last name will be His. Everyone will know that you are a son or a daughter of God.

"That's a child of God," they will say, "an offspring of Jesus Christ. They're supposed to be blessed." Then they'll ask, "What is God like? What does He look like?"

He looks like Jesus.

"Who is Jesus?"

He is God's Son.

"What does He look like?"

Peace. Love. Wisdom.

"What color is He?"

He is like His Father, all light. And in Him there is no darkness at all.

God is illumination, and in Him there is no obscurity. God is clarity. God is revelation. God is truth. And you and I are delivered by the truth of God. Do you want to be blessed? Be obedient to the Lord.

The Lord will open the heavens, the storehouse of his bounties. He will send down upon you the blessings of His will. He'll send rain on your land in season and bless all the work of your hands. You will lend to many nations but borrow from none. The Lord will make you the head and not the tail. If you pay attention and hearken to the commands of the Lord your God and carefully follow them, you will always be at the top and never at the bottom.

Do not turn aside from the many commands of the Lord. Don't turn away.

That's fourteen verses of promises about blessings. And they are all for *you*.

The Curse Vs. the Blessing

However, if you do not obey the Lord your God and do not carefully follow all his commands and decrees I am giving you today, all these curses will come upon you and overtake you.

Deuteronomy 28:15

All this denunciation, all this vilification, all this corruption and disruption and destruction, will come upon you if you are disobedient. It will overtake you. It will accompany you.

You will be cursed in the city and cursed in the country.

Your basket and your kneading trough will be cursed.

The fruit of your womb will be cursed, and the crops of your land, and the calves of your herds and the lambs of your flocks.

You will be cursed when you come in and cursed when you go out.

Deuteronomy 28:16-19

This is the reverse of the blessing.

You will have sons and daughters but you will not keep them, because they will go into captivity.

Deuteronomy 28:41

Your children will be captivated by drugs, alcohol, perversions.

All these curses will come upon you. They will pursue you and overtake you until you are destroyed, because you did not obey the Lord your God and observe the commands and decrees he gave you. They will be a sign and a wonder to you and your descendants forever.

Deuteronomy 28:45,46

Then on through verse 68, the Bible talks about curses for disobedience. Do you know there are many more curses than there are blessings? Because blessings are so potent and complete and powerful you don't need very many of them.

The blessings of God are so wonderful. It doesn't take a whole lot of them to fulfill you. But the curses are aggravating, and there are so many of them.

The Bible says that if we are disobedient, the curse of the Lord will come upon us and overtake us. It will be a sign and a wonder to us and to our descendants forever. We'll look around at America and it will be in shambles, and all the generations following us will say, "Daddy, what did you people do? Granddad, why did you leave us an environment completely destroyed? Why did you leave us drug-infested cities and crime-ridden communities?"

This decade you're going to notice lots of politicians and preachers and judges and police officers who will be exposed as drug addicts.

Our children and grandchildren are going to ask us what happened. What brought this curse upon our country?

Reward for Return to the Lord

... when you and your children return to the Lord your God and obey him with all your heart and with all your soul according to everything I command you today....

The Lord your God will circumcise your hearts and the hearts of your descendants, so that you may love him with all your heart and with all your soul, and live.

Now what I am commanding you today is not too difficult for you or beyond your reach. It is not up in heaven, so that you have to ask, "Who will ascend into heaven to get it and proclaim it to us so we may obey it?" Nor is it beyond the sea, so that you have to ask, "Who will cross the sea to get it and proclaim it to us so we may obey it?" No, the word is very near you; it is in your mouth and in your heart so you may obey it.

Deuteronomy 30:2,6,11-14

The Word of God is very near us. It is in our confession. It is in our mouth. It is in our conversation. And it is in our heart so that we may obey it and live.

Choose Life

See, I set before you today life and prosperity, death and destruction. For I command you today to love the Lord your God, to walk in his ways, and to keep his commands, decrees and laws; then you will live and increase, and the Lord your God will bless you in the land you are entering to possess.

This day I call heaven and earth as witnesses against you that I have set before you life and death, blessings and curses. Now choose life, so that you and your children may live and that you may love the Lord your God, listen to his voice, and hold fast to him. For the Lord is your life, and he will give you many years in the land he swore to give to your fathers....

Deuteronomy 30:15,16,19,20

I have decided I'm not going to be poor all my life. My parents, our community, our people, had a poverty mentality, even though we were in the church. We'd go to church and have the most powerful meetings. We'd shout and jump and cast out devils. But most of the people were poor. We could barely make it.

That is not God's will as described here in this passage from Deuteronomy. God wants us to prosper and be in health even as our soul prospers. (3 John 2.) He wants us to be healthy, happy, and holy, in Jesus.

Jesus said, ''I am come that you might have life, and that you might have it more abundantly.'' (John 10:10.) Jesus came that you and I might be blessed in the cities and in the country — blessed when we go in and when we go out — full of the Holy Ghost — a tree planted by the rivers of water that brings forth fruit.

We will. We can. We are. With God, we win. We're on the winning side. We're sent by God to get our nation back, our city back, our family back, our health back, our mind back. We have declared war on Satan. We are going to tear down his kingdom. We are standing on the edge of the promised land, and we are not thinking about going back. This is not the time for giving up. It's the time for holding on. This is not the time for looking back. It's a time for being strong.

We're not weak. We're strong. Strong in the Lord and in the power of His might. We've got on the whole armor of God. We are able to stand against the wiles of the devil and having done all to stand. Let us stand therefore, secure in the knowledge that God has pronounced His blessing upon us and therefore we will not fail.

2
The Balanced Life

Although I hope to come to you soon, I am writing you these instructions so that, if I am delayed, you will know how people ought to conduct themselves in God's household, which is the church of the living God, the pillar and foundation of the truth.

1 Timothy 3:14,15

This letter is the first of the so-called pastoral letters of Paul. They voice the concern of this precious apostle as a pastor at large for the scattered congregations of believers throughout Asia Minor and all over the known world at that time. They deal with church leadership, correct doctrine, and appropriate conduct.

First Timothy, Second Timothy, and Titus are the final correspondence from Paul that we have in the New Testament. They are the last three letters he wrote. These letters are addressed to individuals, but they have impressive ramifications for the churches everywhere. Two of them are written specifically to Timothy and the other one is written to Titus. But as we read them, they contain overtones that refer to the whole Church.

Proper Christian Conduct

There was a sense of urgency in these letters. Paul now was an aging veteran of the Church. He was seventy years old, give or take a few years. He was going to die. He knew his days were numbered, and he recognized that his work on earth was almost finished.

And yet there was so much more to be done. So he wrote these letters to Timothy, thirty-five or forty years his junior. Timothy had been saved during Paul's second missionary journey. His mother was a powerful Jewish woman. So was his grandmother. His father was Greek. Timothy from birth was somewhat timid and fearful, but after he was born again, he became a loyal disciple of Paul.

So Paul rushed this letter to him. The main theme of this book is found in the fifteenth verse of the third chapter. This is the central message of the entire book:

If I am delayed, you will know how people ought to conduct themselves in God's household....

The *King James Version* says "house." But the original Greek word is closer to the word "household." It refers to God's dwelling, His habitation. It has to do with being in the family of God, in the will of God, in the home of God — which, as Paul went on to note, is the Church of the living God, the pillar and foundation of truth.

This message from Paul to his disciple in the faith had to do with how we conduct ourselves as Christians, our conduct toward God. And how God will conduct Himself toward us, that's also important. The main purpose of the book was to strengthen the hand and resolve of Timothy because Paul knew he would go on to reinforce his charge against false teachers and to give instruction for the functioning of the Church. Paul also wrote to give some personal counsel to Timothy himself.

I want to examine this counsel carefully because it will help us achieve and maintain balance in our dealing with the message of prosperity that is being preached and practiced in the Church today. Despite the truth of abundant prosperity which the Lord has promised to those who are obedient to Him, we must guard against building our whole life or ministry around financial teaching. There's danger in that. Let me give you the balanced side.

The Doctrine of Prosperity

If anyone teaches false doctrines and does not agree to the sound instruction of our Lord Jesus Christ and to godly teaching, he is conceited and understands nothing. He has an unhealthy interest in controversies and arguments about words that result in envy, quarreling, malicious talk, evil suspicions and constant

friction between men of corrupt mind, who have been robbed of the truth and who think that godliness is a means to financial gain.

1 Timothy 6:3-5

The *King James Version* of this passage reads:

If any man teach otherwise, and consent not to wholesome words, even the words of our Lord Jesus Christ, and to the doctrine which is according to godliness;

He is proud, knowing nothing, but doting about questions and strifes of words, whereof cometh envy, strife, railings, evil surmisings,

Perverse disputings of men of corrupt minds, and destitute of the truth, supposing that gain is godliness: from such withdraw thyself.

The word *doctrine* as used in this passage simply means "instruction." Today we use it in a legal sense to refer to the beliefs, teachings, and practices of a church or other religious organization. But we don't want to doctrinalize financial gain.

The Greek word translated *gain* in this passage is *porismos*, which means "furnishing, procuring, money-getting, or acquisition." It is a derivative of the root word *poros*, meaning "a way, or means."

Now let's read Verses 3 and 4 again in that light:

"If anyone teaches false doctrines, making a doctrine of prosperity in the sense that it involves only obtaining money, he has erred."

That doesn't mean that we should not teach on prosperity or give instruction about gain. But we are not to make a doctrine of it, as some do — that's all they teach.

Verses 4 and 5 go on to say that "if anyone teaches false doctrines and does not agree with the sound instruction of our Lord Jesus Christ, and to godly teaching, he is conceited and understands nothing.

"He has an unhealthy interest in controversies. And in arguments that result in quarreling, malicious talk, evil suspicions, and constant friction between men of corrupt mind who have been robbed of the truth and who think that godliness is a means to financial gain.''

That is not to say that godliness is not a means to financial gain. That is not the purpose of godliness, but if you are godly (God-like), you will gain. It comes with the territory and is par for the course.

Godliness With Contentment

But godliness [God-likeness, being in and like Christ] **with contentment is great gain** [great procurement].

1 Timothy 6:6

Godliness *is* great gain, not only monetarily, but in every area of life. But in order to be truly godly, to have genuine holiness, we must learn how to be content with God, whether it profits us materially or not.

In Philippians 4:11,12 Paul also said about contentment:

...for I have learned to be content whatever the circumstances. I know what it is to be in need, and I know what it is to have plenty. I have learned the secret of being content in any and every situation, whether well fed or hungry, whether living in plenty or in want.

If, like the Apostle Paul, we can be content with or without the things of this world — content whether in plenty or in want, content whether well fed or hungry, content regardless of our circumstances — then we are truly blessed and have already received great gain.

As a child, I grew up in fairly obscure surroundings. Although some people thought that because my family was neat and clean we had wealth, we never really had large amounts of money. My father made fifty dollars a week. In those days a man could make fifty or eighty or a hundred dollars a week and still make ends meet. Sometimes it took the whole fifty dollars just to feed the family, so we didn't have a lot. We struggled a great deal. We didn't understand the teaching on prosperity. We had unconsciously taken some kind of a vow to poverty.

Everybody in our church was poor. I remember that some people would literally put a quarter a week in the offering. The ushers would pass the plate and somebody would put a dime, a nickel or even a penny. It was pitiful. Do you remember those days? The saints were just bringing pocket change into the Lord's house.

I remember those old deacons counting the money in the service. They would bring out pens and pencils. There would be a group of people standing around the altar acting as if they were counting out thousands of dollars. Then one of them would say, "Let's see, I believe if we can get sixty cents more, we can round it out to an even number."

I remember as a kid thinking that was so stupid. "There's six of you all standing up there," I thought. "Give a dime apiece." But they might not have had even that much to give, or at least they didn't seem willing to give it.

All the envelopes had "building fund" written on them. In every church I was ever in as a child, there was an eternal building program because the old church buildings were always falling apart. The pastor would get up every Sunday and say, "Don't forget the building fund."

Occasionally I go to those same churches today and things haven't changed one bit. The little offering envelope still has "building fund" written on it. Those people have been building that fund for over forty years. They have more fund than building.

But that was our mentality, a poverty mentality. It's all right to catch the sales, if you find them. Bargain hunting is fine, but if you are not careful, you will get locked into a "bargain" mentality. You'll never pay full price for anything. You'll start thinking that if you are a good wheeler-dealer and can find good deals, you're blessed of the Lord. And you can, but that is not the only way God blesses you.

However, if you get locked into such a mentality, then you're not blessed of the Lord — you're in bondage and error. In fact, you are in just as much error as the person who makes a doctrine of prosperity, thinking that godliness is just a means of acquisition.

We must find the balance between the extremes. Because, again, godliness — with contentment — is great gain.

Investing in Eternity

...we brought nothing into the world, and we can take nothing out of it.

1 Timothy 6:7

The story is told of a very wealthy man, a miser, worth millions of dollars. He counted his money for years and years and didn't spend much of it. But everyone knew he was rich. When he died somebody asked, "How much did he leave?" The answer came back: "He left all of it."

He could take none of it with him.

I don't care how much we acquire and accrue on this earth, we're going to leave all of it here. Only what we do for Christ will be taken with us. So we need to invest our lives seeking after something with more eternal value than stocks and bonds, houses and lands.

Then I heard a voice from heaven say,

"...Blessed are the dead who die in the Lord from now on."

"Yes," says the Spirit, "they will rest from their labor, for their deeds will follow them."

Revelation 14:13

Contentment With Sufficiency

But if we have food and clothing, we will be content with that.

1 Timothy 6:8

This seems overly simplistic, nonetheless it is scriptural. Yet you will hear very few preachers today teaching this truth.

The Balanced Life

People who want to get rich fall into temptation and a trap and into many foolish and harmful desires that plunge man into ruin and destruction. For the love of money [not money itself] **is a root of all kinds of evil. Some people, eager for money, have wandered from the faith and pierced themselves with many griefs.**
1 Timothy 6:9,10

Beloved, there's a very thin line in that passage. I'm going to preach prosperity, the covenant blessing of the Lord. I want you to prosper — and so does God. If you are obedient and faithful, you are going to prosper. But at the same time, we don't want to get so far into the prosperity mentality that we fall into error just as we did when we believed exclusively in the poverty mentality.

We must be careful about getting so far away from a poverty mentality that all we think about is money and homes and cars and shoes and clothes and vacation trips, etc. I want you to have all that. I have some of that. I'm enjoying things as an adult that I only dreamed of as a child. I can afford to get on a plane and fly somewhere and enjoy myself. I can afford to stay at a decent hotel and order pretty much what I want to eat. I don't have to pinch pennies because I am blessed with a decent job and income. I know how to earn money. I'm blessed, but I'm not silly. I don't preach to make a living, I preach because I already live, and because I want others to live, because I want you to live. But I also want us to be balanced in our living and in our whole attitude towards God's prosperity.

Invest in the Kingdom

Do not store up for yourselves treasures on earth, where moth and rust destroy, and where thieves break

**in and steal. But store up for yourselves treasures in
heaven, where moth and rust do not destroy, and
where thieves do not break in and steal. For where
your treasure is, there your heart will be also.**

Matthew 6:19-21

What does Jesus mean in this passage? Does He mean
that we shouldn't have a savings account? It's really
irresponsible not to do so in this day. It's all right to put
a little money aside for saving. I'll be honest with you. I
have difficulty doing that, especially when I know there are
needs in my church or ministry. Jesus said, "Don't store
up treasures for *yourselves.*"

Do you know that there's not a person in our church
who can go into impoverishment as long as he or she is an
active member of our part of the Body of Christ? We would
take care of that individual. That's our godly responsibility,
to take care of the people in our church as well as our family.

One of these days we'd love to have a retirement village
on the grounds for the senior saints when they get old. We
have a responsibility to take care of our parents. All believers
do. That's one good reason to lay aside money — *for the
sake of others* who are dependent on us. So we ought to be
thinking about financial responsibilities like that. We should
save up for such situations. When we store up treasures,
it must be primarily for others rather than ourselves.

I want to teach you how to live a productive life, and
to make sure that you and your loved ones are taken care
of. That is responsible Christian stewardship.

Notice that the Lord spoke of our "treasure." In Greek
the word translated as *treasure* actually means "deposits"
or "values." He said to lay up our treasures, to make our
deposits, in heaven — not on earth — for where our treasure
is, there our heart will be also.

Where do you invest your money? Where's a good
place to invest or deposit your money? I'm sure the Lord
could give us some good and practical advice on that subject.

He said that the Kingdom of God is the best investment on the market. The Kingdom of God is the best place to deposit your treasure. Why? Because moth and rust can't corrupt it there. Robbers can't break in and steal it there.

Now when I speak of the Kingdom of God, I don't mean the church as a building, I mean the invisible Kingdom of God. There is where we should be investing our resources — our money, our time, our lives. We should be investing in things that will advance the spread of the Gospel. Nobody can destroy it there. God will prevent anyone or anything from destroying it. He will protect it and see to it that our needs are met.

The Righteous Are Never Forsaken

The psalmist David said, I was young and now I am old, yet I have never seen the righteous forsaken or their children begging bread (Ps. 37:25). Righteous people are never forsaken and their seed (their offspring) don't beg for food.

Scripture says that where your treasure is, there will your heart be also. If you put money in the work of the Lord, your heart is there, because that's where your treasure is. That's where you have invested that hard-earned cash that you worked for and perspired for. You don't spend eight to twelve hours a day, five to six days a week, fifty weeks out of the year working for nothing. The bulk of your life is spent on the job. Every day. Week in and week out. If you can get two days off for the weekend, you're blessed, and even then you must work on or over what you've earned.

Most of us *have* to work. I really don't have any time off. Those of us in the ministry try to take time off occasionally but there's always something to do, always a need to be met. Even our social gatherings and outings are related to the ministry. Most ministers, pastors in particular, are on call twenty-four hours a day. We're working all the time mending broken lives. But do you know that God blesses us richly for it? The Kingdom of God pays a marvelous dividend to its investors. We enjoy abundant living in so very many ways.

Don't Worry

Therefore I tell you, do not worry about your life, what you will eat or drink; or about your body, what you will wear. . . .

Matthew 6:25

Our Lord commands us not to worry about our life. He did not say that we are not to be concerned. He said, don't *worry* about it. Don't be vexed about it. Don't be fearful about it. Don't be anxious about it.

It's all right to plan what you're going to prepare for your next meal. It's all right to lay out tonight what you're going to wear tomorrow. That's not a sin. But Jesus said that we are not to worry or fret or suffer anxiety about what we're going to eat and drink and wear.

God Will Provide

. . . Is not life more important than food, and the body more important than clothes? Look at the birds of the air; they do not sow or reap or store away in barns, and yet your heavenly Father feeds them. Are you not much more valuable than they?

Matthew 6:25,26

God takes care of the birds of the air. What makes us think that He will not meet our needs as well? Do we really think that He cares more for birds than He does for us? Absolutely not.

Many of us have pets, a dog or cat that we feed and house and take care of. Do we think that we are better providers for our household pets than God is for His own beloved children whom He suffered and died for? Again, absolutely not!

Worry Is Fruitless

Who of you by worrying can add a single hour to his life?

Matthew 6:27

In most cases the only thing worry, stress, and hard work do is take hours, or even years, from our life.

Here Jesus echoed the words of the psalmist who wrote: **In vain you rise up early and stay up late, toiling for food to eat — for he grants sleep to those he loves** (Ps. 127:2). A footnote in the *New International Bible* gives an alternate translation of this last statement: ''...for while they sleep, He provides for those He loves.'' While we sleep (in other words, in our rest or peace, which really means calm resolve) God is taking care of our every need **...according to his glorious riches in Christ Jesus** (Phil. 4:19).

First Things First

And why do you worry about clothes? See how the lilies of the field grow. They do not labor or spin. Yet I tell you that not even Solomon in all his splendor was dressed like one of these.

If that is how God clothes the grass of the field, which is here today and tomorrow is thrown into the fire, will he not much more clothe you, O you of little faith?

So do not worry, saying, ''What shall we eat?'' or ''What shall we drink?'' or ''What shall we wear?'' For the pagans run after all these things, and your heavenly Father knows that you need them. But seek first his kingdom and his righteousness, and all these things will be given to you as well.

Matthew 6:28-33

First things first. We are to seek first the Kingdom of God and His righteousness, and then all these things that we need — clothes and food for the body and a roof over our head and somebody to love and be loved by — all of these things will be added unto us as well. God knows we are dependent upon them for our very existence.

According to Romans 14:17 ...**the kingdom of God is not a matter of eating and drinking, but of righteousness, peace and joy in the Holy Spirit.** The Kingdom of God is not a matter of what we eat or drink or wear; it isn't a religious matter at all. It is a matter of righteousness, peace, and joy in the Holy Ghost. That's what we are to seek. That's what we are to run after: righteousness, peace, and joy in the Holy Ghost.

One Day at a Time

Therefore do not worry about tomorrow, for tomorrow will worry about itself. Each day has enough trouble of its own.

Matthew 6:34

This is Jesus talking. Do you believe He means exactly what He says? **Cast all your anxiety on him because he cares for you** (1 Pet. 5:7).

3
Practical Prosperity

Let's look at a few of the characteristics in the book of First Timothy as we discuss an even more practical approach to biblical prosperity.

Here is a trustworthy saying: If anyone sets his heart on being an overseer, he desires a noble task. Now the overseer must be above reproach....

1 Timothy 3:1,2

Here the Apostle Paul is instructing his young disciple, Timothy, in the qualities required of an overseer or bishop in the Church. As we will see, he stresses that morally, ethically, and domestically, the overseer must be of the highest caliber. I think that for the most part these basic disciplines apply to all Christians in general. Let's go a little further.

Monogamous

...the husband of but one wife....

1 Timothy 3:2

In Paul's day, it was permissible in many cultures to have more than one wife. But in Christian circles, this was not allowed, especially among those who were spiritual leaders. No man who desired to be a leader in the Church could be involved in a polygamous relationship.

Self-Controlled

...temperate, self-controlled, respectable, hospitable, able to teach, not given to much wine....

1 Timothy 3:2,3

The spiritual leader was to be exemplary in his behavior and deportment. He was to be self-controlled. He was to be worthy of respect. He was to be warm and hospitable to others. He was to be teachable. And he was to be moderate in his personal habits including eating and drinking.

Interestingly enough, although we discourage people from drinking alcoholic beverages at all, the Bible never actually fully denounces drinking. (Personally, I don't drink. I don't even drink out of a glass that looks like a cocktail glass because I don't want to give the appearance of doing evil.) In many areas of the world, people are going to drink. It's just part of the culture, the way they were reared. It's nothing more or less than a custom.

I was brought up to believe that a Christian doesn't drink, smoke, tip, dip, or sip. If someone did any of those things, we just knew he was going to hell. That's the way we were taught in our culture and society. But in the early days of the Church, it was accepted that people, even believers, were going to drink wine — in moderation.

In fact, part of Paul's instruction to Timothy in this same letter was, **Stop drinking only water, and use a little wine because of your stomach and your frequent illnesses** (1 Tim. 5:23). But Paul also made it clear that a spiritual leader was not to be one who was an abuser of alcohol.

Not a Lover of Money

. . . not violent but gentle, not quarrelsome, not a lover of money.

1 Timothy 3:3

Obviously a spiritual leader should not be a violent, ill-tempered person, one who engages in quarrels, arguments, and needless controversies. He should also not be a "lover of money."

This raises some interesting questions: How should the preacher live? Should he take a vow of poverty? Should he preach prosperity and live in poverty? No. But he shouldn't live like a multi-millionaire either. If he inherits a lot of money, he can live as comfortably as he wants to. However, while Christians are "King's kids," and should live as such, a preacher must not do so on the fruits of other people's hard labor. In fact, if he receives a huge inheritance, he should set aside enough to live comfortably, and then give the rest to the work of the Lord.

I feel very confident that I could earn a good income from engagements outside my church. I know I could earn significant amounts by just speaking. I could put it all in my pocket. I could hire a secretary who could book me all over the country and abroad. I could take musicians with me. I wouldn't have to take singers because I can sing myself. I could walk out of the church and go my own way. I could live the rest of my life, as long as the Lord blesses me, and live very comfortably. I could give wherever I wanted to give. But I won't do that. Instead, I choose to stay where I am and serve, to share my life and my limited financial means with the people God has given me. And I make a comfortable living doing that. Because the more I give, the more I have to give. Nevertheless I know how to be a good steward of the money which the Lord provides me. Some ministers do not. Money causes a lot of preachers to fall. They begin to see all those dollars coming into their ministry as theirs to put into their pocket or to use to build their own personal kingdoms instead of furthering the Kingdom of God. That's the danger that the Apostle Paul is warning against here in this passage.

A Capable Manager

He must manage his own family well and see that his children obey him with proper respect. (If anyone does not know how to manage his own family, how can he take care of God's church?)

1 Timothy 3:4,5

Again, this is not just for bishops. Really this instruction is for everybody. This applies to all Christians in one sense. If a person does not know how to manage his own family, how can he take care of God's Church? It's wrong for the preacher's kids to be the worst ones in the church. We must learn to make our children the most respectable in town. The way we treat and teach them at home will determine how they act outside the home. Our children are not our fault. They are our responsibility.

Humble and Reputable

He must not be a recent convert, or he may become conceited and fall under the same judgment as the devil [which was pride]. He must also have a good reputation with outsiders, so that he will not fall into disgrace and into the devil's trap.

1 Timothy 3:6,7

In other words, a leader or a Christian should not be prideful, vain, arrogant, or conceited. He must also pay his bills, and pay them on time. He shouldn't owe everybody in town, or if he does, he must make consistent and regular payments toward them all in good faith.

As believers, we should have a reputation of paying our bills and taking care of our affairs. Our house and yard should be the best kept on the block. Our clothes should be clean and pressed. We should be well groomed. Our children should be well mannered, polite, and industrious, not necessarily the smartest but the *best* students in school. We should be examples of the finest citizens in the society. People should know that we are of God, and that Jesus is our Lord.

Respectable, Not Money Hungry

Deacons, likewise, are to be men worthy of respect, sincere, not indulging in much wine, and not pursuing dishonest gain.

1 Timothy 3:8

When addressing the subject of ministers, for whatever reason, money is always something which finds its way into the conversation. It is mentioned in reference to the bishop. Here Paul speaks of it when listing the qualities required of a deacon. He says that they too must be men who are respectable, sincere, self-controlled, not intent on pursuing dishonest gain. Evidently mammon, money, or "filthy lucre," as the *King James Version* refers to it, must have always been a strong temptation in the Church.

Faithful, Tested

They must keep hold of the deep truths of the faith with a clear conscience. They must first be tested; and then if there is nothing against them, let them serve as deacons.

1 Timothy 3:9,10

Paul says that deacons are to be tested. The same applies to bishops, pastors, and any others who serve the Lord in His Church. No one has a right to fill a position of spiritual leadership who refuses to submit to the scrutiny and authority of the church and its officials.

The Deacon's Wife

In the same way, their wives are to be women worthy of respect, not malicious talkers but temperate and trustworthy in everything.

1 Timothy 3:11

Women must be worthy of respect — *not malicious talkers*. A wife of a spiritual leader should respect her husband and his position in the church. She should support him by her words, attitude, and actions. She should keep careful control over what goes out of her mouth, especially as it relates to the Body of Christ or persons within it.

Good and Faithful Servants

A deacon must be the husband of but one wife and must manage his children and his household well. Those who have served well gain an excellent standing and great assurance in their faith in Christ Jesus.

Although I hope to come to you soon, I am writing you these instructions so that, if I am delayed, you will know how people ought to conduct themselves in God's household, which is the church of the living God, the pillar and foundation of the truth.

1 Timothy 3:12-15

Here Paul concludes his description of the qualities of spiritual leaders, urging young Timothy to heed and observe his instructions which set forth the rules of proper conduct for those who occupy positions of responsibility and authority in the Church of Jesus Christ, the pillar and foundation of truth.

Until I Come...

Until I come, devote yourself to the public reading of Scripture, to preaching and to teaching. Do not neglect your gift, which was given you through a prophetic message when the body of elders laid their hands on you.

Be diligent in these matters; give yourself wholly to them, so that everyone may see your progress. Watch your life and doctrine closely. Persevere in them, because if you do, you will save both yourself and your hearers.

1 Timothy 4:13-16

Every teacher, every preacher, ought to be concerned not only about saving himself, but about saving his hearers. He should be careful to watch his life and doctrine, his teaching and instruction. His spiritual progress should be visible and obvious to all.

I am a better person this year than I was last year. I have read more books. I've expanded my thinking. I'm more intelligent, more alert, more sensitive, more spiritual. I'm more anointed. I have better control over my temper. I watch my life and my instruction.

I have improved not only mentally and spiritually but physically as well. I'm eating better. I've lost weight. I feel better about myself. I can breathe better. It's important to feel good about yourself. Like Paul, I whip (discipline) myself when I get out of line. Paul said that he beat his body and made it his slave so that after he had preached to others he himself would not be disqualified for the prize. (1 Cor. 9:27.)

Since I have gotten control of my mind and body and spirit, I must work every day to maintain the control; as

54

a result, I am better able to take the strain of this kind of work. You have no idea the stress a pastor goes through in a week. You don't know the letters and phone calls and confrontations we face. So I have to rest and eat well because the stress will kill me if I don't.

Paul knew these things. That's why he is counseling young Timothy on how to cope with the demands of spiritual leadership. He is also giving him sound advice on how to deal with the people in his charge.

Dealing With the Elderly

Do not rebuke an older man harshly, but exhort him as if he were your father....

1 Timothy 5:1

Notice the respect that Paul suggests a leader have for the elderly. In my ministry, I am very careful to heed that instruction. I treat all my elders with the respect and deference that is due persons of their age, knowledge, and experience. Treating elders or the elderly with special respect and regard is a customary practice of most ethnic cultures — it should remain so indefinitely.

Dealing With Young People and Older Women

...Treat younger men as brothers, older women as mothers, and younger women as sisters, with absolute purity.

1 Timothy 5:1,2

Younger men should be treated as brothers, younger women as sisters in Christ — with absolute purity of mind and heart.

Every older woman in the church should be treated as a mother. The gentlemen of the church should open the door for her, pull a chair out for her, help her to her car. Someone should see to it that the older ladies of the church have food to eat, clean clothes to wear, adequate transportation wherever they might need to go, plenty of heating fuel in the winter — all the things that we would do for our own mothers and grandmothers.

Dealing With Widows in Need

Give proper recognition to those widows who are really in need. But if a widow has children or grandchildren, these should learn first of all to put their religion into practice by caring for their own family and so repaying their parents and grandparents, for this is pleasing to God. The widow who is really in need and left all alone puts her hope in God and continues night and day to pray and to ask God for help. But the widow who lives for pleasure is dead even while she lives.

1 Timothy 5:3-6

We in the church are to take care of our own parents and grandparents. We are to help others of our church who are in need, but first we want to know where their family members are. Where is the widow's family? Why are they not caring for her as they should? There are a lot of young widows. Their husbands die young, and these young ladies live for pleasure. These we are not obligated to assist. We turn them over to the Holy Spirit's power to convict and save.

Dealing With Dependents

Give the people these instructions, too, so that no one may be open to blame. If anyone does not provide for his relatives, and especially for his immediate family, he has denied the faith and is worse than an unbeliever [or infidel].

1 Timothy 5:7,8

As a pastor, I've got to look after my own family. Not necessarily at the expense of my congregation, but I must see after them nonetheless. I have a younger sister. She's the youngest child in our family. I have to look out for her. I care about where she goes, who she goes with, what time she gets in at night. I care about what she wears. And as long as she's living in my house, she is going to have to be under my supervision and authority. When she moves out or gets married, I will still care, but my responsibility will cease.

She takes good care of my house. She can cook. She doesn't always do it, but she can. She cleans, and she manages things. She turns back the bed for me. She makes sure I drink plenty of water, and she tries to see that I get my vitamins.

We look after and care for each other because that's our desire — and our Christian duty. We don't expect the church to do for us what we are to do for ourselves. No minister or pastor should.

The Widows' List

No widow may be put on the list of widows unless she is over sixty, has been faithful to her husband, and is well-known for her good deeds, such as bringing up children, showing hospitality, washing the feet of the saints, helping those in trouble and devoting herself to all kinds of good deeds.

1 Timothy 5:9,10

I tell the widows of our congregation to remember this passage. I assure them that if they are ever in need we will be there for them. We will add their names to the list of deserving widows. But I also point out that not just anybody can get on the list. They've got to be people who have meant something to our fellowship.

We are not responsible to care for another widow in the same way we are charged to if the widow has been faithful to the church.

Dealing With Younger Widows

As for younger widows, do not put them on such a list. For when their sensual desires overcome their dedication to Christ, they want to marry. Thus they

bring judgment on themselves, because they have broken their first pledge.

1 Timothy 5:11,12

I warn the young women of our church not to run around quickly saying, "I'm married to Jesus," because it is not realistic. As long as a woman is young, she is not married to anybody. She shouldn't fool herself or psyche herself out. If she wants to marry, she can. But she shouldn't make a premature vow that she may not keep. To do so is to bring judgment on herself because she is in danger of breaking her first pledge, which is to be celibate and dedicated only to the Lord.

A woman can be holy without claiming that she is married to Jesus. That claim impresses no one.

Besides, they get into the habit of being idle and going from house to house. And not only do they become idlers, but also gossips and busybodies, saying things they ought not to.

1 Timothy 5:13

This is very practical teaching. We need it. What does it have to do with prosperity? It affects the spirit, which has a direct bearing on a person's well being — in every aspect of life and prosperous living.

So I counsel younger widows to marry, to have children, to manage their homes and to give the enemy no opportunity for slander. Some have in fact already turned away to follow Satan.

1 Timothy 5:14,15

I counsel the young women of our church (and of course this advice applies to young men as well) not to associate exclusively with other people their own age. I urge them to enjoy fellowshipping also with more mature and serious people as well. I teach them to do things that are fun and recreational, but things that challenge and stretch them so they grow.

Take Care of Your Own

If any woman who is a believer has widows in her family, she should help them and not let the church be burdened with them, so that the church can help those widows who are really in need.
1 Timothy 5:16

Can't you see how these scriptures relate to your prosperity? They are practical and applicable to individuals as well as to the Church Body of believers at large. The church itself and membership in it is a form of prosperity to each parishioner.

The Worker Deserves His Wages

The elders who direct the affairs of the church well are worthy of double honor, especially those whose work is preaching and teaching. For the Scripture says, "Do not muzzle the ox while it is treading out the grain," and "The worker deserves his wages."
1 Timothy 5:17,18

Here Paul says the preacher should be paid well.

Don't say, "All these preachers are going around living off the people; they're doing better than anybody else in the church." Usually it is the rich who say that. The sweetest folks are usually the poorest folks. They give, and they're happy that somebody is using their gifts to further the Kingdom of God. It's the ones who have all the money — those who can live any way they want to live, drive anything they want to drive, go any place they want to go — who don't want the preacher to have anything.

Paul said to Timothy that the ones who direct the affairs of the church well are worthy of *double* honor, especially those whose work is preaching and teaching.

Dealing With Those Who Sin

Do not entertain an accusation against an elder unless it is brought by two or three witnesses. Those

who sin are to be rebuked publicly, so that the others may take warning.

1 Timothy 5:19,20

Here Paul is referring to those who have been dealt with privately and who have not responded. If they continue to sin, they must be rebuked publicly. I have a specific teaching on this subject that goes into much more detail, but we'll save that for another discussion.

Keep These Instructions
— and Prosper!

I charge you, in the sight of God and Christ Jesus and the elect angels, to keep these instructions without partiality, and to do nothing out of favoritism.

1 Timothy 5:21

These verses from First Timothy we have examined in this chapter are just basic teaching about the Christian life and conduct. It has a direct bearing on our mental, physical, and spiritual prosperity.

When I say that God wills health, happiness, and holiness for His children, I mean it. I mean that He wants to share with us practical ways of living. Young people, older people, middle-aged people — this applies to all of us.

I'm going to make you a promise, and I know it's of God. You are about to be blessed and visited by the Lord. This is going to sound presumptuous, what I'm about to write. But right now, please understand the spirit in which I write this. I know that I am called and I know that I am anointed. I know that I am a man of destiny and that I am on assignment. So please hear and receive this word from the Lord.

God's hand is on us. It's wonderful. We are on the cutting edge of what's going to change the face of this nation. We're one of the voices that will be heard if we continue with God as we are. Ours may be one of the last voices heard on a global scale before the second coming of the Lord.

I wish I could describe to you the incredible doors of opportunity that are opening to us right now and the anointing that rests upon us. God has punctuated our lives with His anointing. The blessing of the Lord is on us.

You are blessed. Your church is blessed. Whatever you do is going to be blessed of the Lord — if you keep your heart pure and your spirit humble, and if you know who you are. You are about to be blessed in a special way. I believe God is going to bless you spiritually, mentally, domestically. Start expecting wonderful things to happen in your life. Have faith in God. And watch what the Holy Spirit does.

Start expecting to be happy in your marriage. Start expecting to pay off your bills. Start expecting to be anointed to speak and think. If you are in school, in business, or in the ministry, start expecting to do well. Think upward. Think productively.

Believe in yourself. I believe in you. I believe in this word which the Lord has given me for you. I believe this is the prophetic hour for the Church.

Some people think we are an overnight success. No such thing. I have been at this for over thirty years. Dreaming, even at times fantasizing, about ministering.

When I was fasting and planning for thirty days in my thirtieth year, 1983, the Lord spoke to me and told me to get up and watch the sunrise. As I wearily waited for what seemed like hours to see the sun make its appearance over the eastern horizon, He said to me, "There are no quick sunrises. One of these days before the world really recognizes what I'm going to do, you'll be like a sun ball blazing in the sky, and folks will say you're an overnight success. But you'll know the price that was paid and the cost."

So the Lord has already told me that it will be a slow sunrise. But when it does come, people are going to call it an overnight success. Only I will know in my heart that there is no such thing as an overnight success. In fact, most people don't even know that success is based on the Lord's standards. Success is not a destination, it's a journey. It's not a coronation, it's a systematic developmental and evolutionary process.

I don't know how to arrive. I only know how to keep on going. We're going to keep on going. It takes time to be holy. Let the Holy Ghost irrigate and lubricate you. Let the waters of the Spirit moisturize your life and believe. The sun will rise, and you will prosper — in God's time.

4

Prepared to Prosper

Now to him who is able to do immeasurably more than all we ask or imagine, according to his power that is at work within us, to him be glory in the church and in Christ Jesus throughout all generations, for ever and ever! Amen.

Ephesians 3:20,21

Our God is an able God. He is able to do immeasurably more than we ask or desire or need. Able to do far more than we can ever think or even imagine.

The Lord has been dealing with me about asking and imagining. The problem the Holy Spirit helped me to see is that our imagery is sometimes in contrast to our asking. We're not asking what we're thinking. Or we're not thinking what we're asking.

The Lord is going to show us how to synthesize the asking and the thinking so that we may enjoy the "immeasurably more" that He is able to do.

God has said for us to change our asking and our thinking. We are to make sure that our asking and our thinking are in line with His will. And when we are asking and thinking in line with what God is saying and doing, we're on the right track; then no weapon formed against us can prosper. (Isa. 54:17 KJV.) In order to begin to get our asking and thinking in proper perspective, let's go back to Deuteronomy, Chapter 8, to see what Moses told the children of Israel before he gave them God's great promise of blessing and abundance.

Humbled and Tested

Be careful to follow every command I am giving you today, so that you may live and increase and may enter and possess the land that the Lord promised on oath to your forefathers. Remember how the Lord your God led you all the way in the desert these forty years,

**to humble you and to test you in order to know what
was in your heart, whether or not you would keep his
commands.**

Deuteronomy 8:1,2

When I think of my Classical Pentecostal background,
I am reminded that most of it was in the midst of poverty.
We were uneducated and impoverished. I think that
perhaps God let me grow up that way to test my heart, to
find out what I'm made of, to see if I could be trusted with
prosperity later on.

When I was growing up, Christians didn't have the
prosperity message and mentality that we do today. We
thought that Christians were supposed to be poor and
humble. If you were a believer, you weren't supposed to
even expect a nice house and clothes and cars. We were
the dispossessed over in the corner. We didn't have
anything and had fairly well learned to be content to do
without.

Some time ago my team members and I were in a
meeting in Chicago where we were treated royally. We were
picked up at the airport in a chauffeur-driven limousine and
taken to a five-star downtown hotel where we were booked
into a luxury suite. We were served delicious meals. It was
wonderful.

As I enjoyed all that luxury, I remembered my younger
days and thought that all my upbringing had been to
humble me and to prepare me to handle the wonderful
abundance that is being poured out on me now. So far I'm
handling it quite well through the grace and help of the Holy
Spirit.

Don't Forget

**He humbled you, causing you to hunger and then
feeding you with manna, which neither you nor your
fathers had known, to teach you that man does not live
on bread alone but on every word that comes from the**

**mouth of the Lord. Your clothes did not wear out and
your feet did not swell during these forty years.**
Deuteronomy 8:3,4

Again, as a child growing up, I wanted some of my
clothes to wear out so I could get some new ones. We had
to wear hand-me-downs. But as in the case of the Israelites,
God seemed to fix it so our clothes would last for
generations. I always hated that.

I remember one time we did get some new shoes. In
those times, in the late '50s and early '60s, fashionable blacks
wore black shiny shoes with pointy toes and very high heels.
My father didn't necessarily care about style. He wanted
something that would last. He would buy us children shoes
that tied up and had thick durable soles.

I cried, "Daddy, please don't make me wear these
things."

"Boy, you get those shoes on and keep them on."

I was so depressed at school. At recess, instead of
playing with the other children, I'd take off those bulky
shoes and rub them on the asphalt trying to wear them out.
But God wouldn't let those shoes wear out because He
knew that Mama and Daddy couldn't afford to buy any
more for six children.

My sisters wore great big black and white oxfords, and
they hated them. The other kids said that they looked like
they were wearing cows on their feet. And those big old
shoes would never wear out. You could kick a hole in a wall
with them and not even leave a scratch on them.

Today as I think back, I realize that God was helping,
training, and teaching us, just as He did with the children
of Israel. He was telling us, "Don't forget Me when you
get to the place where you can afford several pairs of nice
shoes, when you get to the place where you can buy new
clothes, when you get to the place where I shower blessings
down on you. Don't forget those hand-me-down clothes
and ugly shoes you used to wear. Don't forget that I was

there and that I sustained you then and will sustain you now, but you must depend on Me.''

The Lord's Discipline

Know then in your heart that as a man disciplines his son, so the Lord your God disciplines you.
Deuteronomy 8:5

God disciplines His children.

The Lord is about to visit His people with special blessings. I promise you that God's abundant blessing is about to fall on His Church in an extraordinary way. When it does, don't forget Him. When you are living in a finer home and driving a nicer car and wearing better clothes, don't forget Who has provided all that for you. Remember that you have all those wonderful things to enjoy only because God wants to put you on display, on exhibition, to let the world know He blesses His people who follow His commands.

Remember the Lord Your God

Observe the commands of the Lord your God, walking in his ways and revering him. For the Lord your God is bringing you into a good land — a land with streams and pools of water, with springs flowing in the valleys and hills; a land with wheat and barley, vines and fig trees, pomegranates, olive oil and honey; a land where bread will not be scarce and you will lack nothing; a land where the rocks are iron and you can dig copper out of the hills.

When you have eaten and are satisfied, praise the Lord your God for the good land he has given you. Be careful that you do not forget the Lord your God, failing to observe his commands, his laws and his decrees that I am giving you this day. Otherwise, when you eat and are satisfied, when you build fine houses and settle down, and when your herds and flocks grow large and your silver and gold increase and all you have

**is multiplied, then your heart will become proud and
you will forget the Lord your God....**
Deuteronomy 8:6-14

God wants to bless you, but if you forget the Lord, He
is not going to continue to make you prosperous because
to do so would be at the expense of your soul. If you have
to live in poverty and wear old clothes and drive a worn-
out car, that is better than being rich and forgetting the Lord.

Be careful that you do not forget the Lord. Both your
soul and material wealth are at stake.

In the End

**...who brought you out of Egypt [out of sin], out
of the land of slavery [or enslavement to poverty]. He
led you through the vast and dreadful desert, that
thirsty and waterless land, with its venomous snakes
and scorpions. He brought you water out of hard rock.
He gave you manna to eat in the desert, something
your fathers had never known, to humble and to test
you so that in the end it might go well with you.**
Deuteronomy 8:14-16

I thank the Lord for my upbringing and formation, for
everything I went through as a child and as a young man.
Although I wouldn't want to relive all of that, I'm still very
grateful that God taught me discipline and holiness as a
youth. I am glad I was raised in a strict environment. We
thought we weren't entitled to much, that we were
supposed to live with lack. We didn't have a lot of especially
nice things, but we didn't necessarily know it, and we took
care of what we did have and were always grateful for it.
Now that we've come out of that poverty mentality, we can
appreciate and take care of what we have today.

It doesn't matter what the Lord wants to give me today;
because of my upbringing and instruction, I believe I can
handle it, whether much or little.

The Lord wants to give you blessings and prosperity,
but He doesn't want it to cause you to lose your soul. He
wants to be sure that you can handle what He is about to

pour out upon you. That's why you are being humbled and tested, so that in the end He can bless you abundantly. And you can bring glory to His name.

The Covenant Confirmed

> **You may say to yourself, "My power and the strength of my hands have produced this wealth for me." But remember the Lord your God, for it is he who gives you the ability** [the power, vigor or force] **to produce wealth, and so confirms his covenant, which he swore to your forefathers, as it is today.**
>
> **Deuteronomy 8:17,18**

The confirmation of the covenant is the ability to produce. The Hebrew word translated *produce* in the NIV of this passage also means "to exhibit or display." (The *King James Version* says "to get.") God is not ashamed of you. He wants to put you on display. He wants to hold you up as an exhibit. You should look holy and act holy and feel holy and be holy. And when people are around you, they should feel that way, too.

I don't say this braggadociously, but many times people say to my team members and me, "What is it about you guys? You are the nicest people." Flight attendants say that to us — it doesn't matter whether we're in coach, first class, or economy. And we've been in all three at different times. Whether we're in fine restaurants or at McDonald's, it doesn't make any difference. We always let Jesus shine. And when the people see Jesus, they ask us, "What do you guys do? There's something about you, a charisma, a warmth. Do you perform?"

We say, "No, we're preachers, we're evangelists, ministers of the Gospel."

God's hand is on us. God's anointing is on us. Whether we are ministering in a huge, successful church or in a small, struggling church, we look and act the same. We treat everyone — rich and poor, young and old, black and white — exactly the same.

God is no respecter of persons. He will bless you if you're black, white, brown, yellow, or red.

Our time has come as believers. God wants to shower down blessings upon His people. You have been through the wilderness. You've wandered long enough. Now get ready to cross over and receive the promises of God. You're tired of enduring, you're ready to conquer. You're going from miracles of endurance to miracles of prosperity, victory, and conquest.

You're leaving the old. You are about to be blessed. God is going to visit you. All you have to do is obey Him.

Love the Lord. Serve Him with all your heart. He is going to send glorious rain on you. Have you been through a dry time? Are you ready for God to send the rain? I don't know about you, but I feel like Elijah who said, "I hear the sound of the abundance of rain" (1 Kings 18:41 KJV).

It's going to rain. Get your bucket out. The Lord is going to fill it up.

A Strict Warning

If you ever forget the Lord your God and follow other gods and worship and bow down to them, I testify against you today that you will surely be destroyed. Like the nations the Lord destroyed before you, so you will be destroyed for not obeying the Lord your God.

Deuteronomy 8:19,20

This is a repetitious warning to us that no matter how much God blesses us in the future, we must be careful to be faithful to Him and to follow all His decrees and commands. Look at what He says to us in the next chapter.

Hear, O Israel

Hear, O Israel. You are now about to cross the Jordan to go in and dispossess nations greater and

**stronger than you, with large cities that have walls up
to the sky.**

Deuteronomy 9:1

"Hear, O people of God." I consider this a prophetic
word for my generation of church leadership and followers
today. We in the Church of Jesus Christ are about to cross
over into the land of special prosperity. We are going to
dispossess nations, unseat and dethrone cultures and
lifestyles and customs greater and stronger than we. We
are going to take over and occupy large cities — cities
(spiritual organisms) physically, technologically, politically,
and financially larger than we are — cities with walls up
to the sky.

Who Can Stand Against Evil?

**The people are strong and tall — Anakites! You
know about them and have heard it said: "Who can
stand up against the Anakites?"**

Deuteronomy 9:2

"Who can stand against the present world systems?"

God's glory is about to come upon us, and we are going
to stand strong and tall against incumbent spiritual powers.
We're going to unseat them and dethrone them under
God's anointing.

The Lord Goes Ahead of You

**But be assured today that the Lord your God is
the one who goes across ahead of you like a devouring
fire. He will destroy them; he will subdue them before
you. And you will drive them out and annihilate them
quickly, as the Lord has promised you.**

Deuteronomy 9:3

The Hebrew word translated *drive* in this verse suggests
that the Lord will *overthrow* the inhabitants of this region.
He will desolate them. The *King James Version* says that God
will "bring them down." He will *subdue* them or *undo* them
before us, then we will drive them out. The word indicates
to disinherit by expulsion.

We're going to expel bad spirits from our communities. We're going to cast out evil spirits from our neighborhoods. We're going to unseat demonic strongholds, casting down imaginations, and every high thing that exalts itself against the knowledge of God. Because the weapons of our warfare are not carnal, but mighty through God, we're going to pull down, unseat, and dethrone all kinds of evil spirits. We're going to run them out of town. We're going to annihilate them.

The spirit of extermination is going to come upon God's courageous people. The power of God is going to come upon you, and you're going to be able to look at your own family and rule out everything that doesn't belong there. You're going to be able to look at your own business and unseat those bad spirits. You're going to be able to look at your ministry or church and cast out every unclean spirit that has been dominating it in the past.

Not By Our Righteousness

After the Lord your God has driven them out before you, do not say to yourself, "The Lord has brought me here to take possession of this land because of my righteousness." No, it is on account of the wickedness of these nations that the Lord is going to drive them out before you. It is not because of your righteousness or your integrity that you are going in to take possession of their land; but on account of the wickedness of these nations, the Lord your God will drive them out before you, to accomplish what he swore to your fathers, to Abraham, Isaac and Jacob. Understand, then, that it is not because of your righteousness that the Lord your God is giving you this good land to possess, for you are a stiff-necked people.

Deuteronomy 9:4-6

It is not because of our righteousness or our integrity that we are going to take possession of the land, but on account of the wickedness of those who occupy it.

71

The Lord is saying to us here, ''I'm going to drive out what is before you in the land I am giving you as an inheritance because I hate evil. You are going to go in and take possession of this good land because I love you and have chosen to put My name upon you and My Spirit or power among you. You will enter this land by inheritance, but you will maintain it by obedience.''

To state it another way, the gifts of the Spirit will open the doors, but the fruits of the Spirit will keep them open.

5
Enter and Overcome

When the Lord your God brings you into the land
you are entering to possess and drives out before you
many nations — the Hittites, Girgashites, Amorites,
Canaanites, Perizzites, Hivites and Jebusites, seven
nations larger and stronger than you — and when the
Lord your God has delivered them over to you and you
have defeated them, then you must destroy them
totally....

Deuteronomy 7:1,2

Prophetically speaking, I believe the Lord is going to
allow the controls of certain ungodly systems to come into
our hands. Let's not compromise. We must maintain our
integrity and follow His specific and explicit directions.

We never know what God is going to provide for us
through others. People are liable to literally give us
buildings, property, radio stations, television stations,
airplanes, helicopters, boats — anything we need to fulfill
our godly purpose in the earth. I don't know about you,
but I'm ready to receive from God. I've been through the
wilderness long enough. I've been wandering long enough.
It's now time to cross over into the land of promise.

I've been in debt long enough. I've been impoverished
long enough. I've been under the weight of the strain long
enough. I'm ready to pay my bills and buy my home and
more effectively minister, free from financial restraints. I'm
crossing over to the other side.

I can't go under because I'm going over. Won't you
join me?

Make No Compromise With Evil

Make no treaty with them, and show them no
mercy. Do not intermarry with them. Do not give your
daughters to their sons or take their daughters for your
sons, for they will turn your sons away from following

73

> me to serve other gods, and the Lord's anger will burn
> against you and will quickly destroy you.
> Deuteronomy 7:2b-4

When the children of Israel entered their promised land, they had to face seven tribes or nations that were larger and stronger than they. In verse 1 of this passage, the Lord identifies those seven nations, which I think represented these seven spirits, warning the Israelites that they must not compromise with them, but that they must utterly destroy them.

When we enter into our twenty-first century inheritance (spiritually and historically), we, too, will have to face spirits which must be destroyed totally and completely. That's part of our deliverance. We must make no treaty with them, no alliance. We must not allow a foreign spirit of any kind to enter into our mind and heart. We must refuse to negotiate a deal with them. We must cast them out, showing them no mercy.

I have heard demons speak though an individual and plead for mercy to the point that I almost felt sorry for them. I have heard them change their voice like a child, crying to me personally for mercy. Demons have pleaded with me, and I have let them exist at times. Demons played a mind game with me and drew my sympathy and tricked me. Never again. I will show them no mercy.

When demons cower down and literally whimper like a child, begging you to let them exist, you must mercilessly cast them out. Strangle them and paralyze their influence on your own life. Do not intermarry (betroth) them or even intermingle with them. Have no intimacy with them. Enter no coalition with them. Do not give your daughters to their sons or take their daughters for your sons.

Don't let the things that God produces in you sleep with other spirits. Don't let the gifts of God in you enter into procreation with other cultures or spirits. For they will turn your sons (your own spiritual offspring), the thing that bears your name and nature, away from following the Lord to serve other gods. As a result, the Lord's anger will burn against you and will quickly destroy you.

This is a severe warning which we would do well to heed.

A Holy People

This is what you are to do to them: Break down their altars, smash their sacred stones, cut down their Asherah poles and burn their idols in the fire. For you are a people holy to the Lord your God. The Lord your God has chosen you out of all the peoples on the face of the earth to be his people, his treasured possession.
Deuteronomy 7:5,6

As the people of God, we are to be on guard against spirits — habits, hobbies, hungers, values, and priorities — that are not of God. We must destroy these images, cutting down these spiritual poles which are symbolic of worship of false gods. We must burn their idols in the fire, the fire of our own faith, the fire of our own courage. For we are a holy nation, separated to the Lord our God Who has chosen us out of all the tribes on the face of the earth to be His people, His treasured possession.

The *King James Version* of this passage says that we are His "special people," the same thought expressed by Peter when he wrote: **But ye are a chosen generation, a royal priesthood, an holy nation, a peculiar people...**(1 Pet. 2:9 KJV). A better translation is "a treasured possession."

Literally, Deuteronomy 7 was addressed to the Jews. If we are going to read this passage and spiritualize it for New Testament reference and significance, we would have to apply it to anybody who has been baptized into Jesus Christ and has become an heir to the promise of Abraham. (Gal. 3:26-28.)

Spiritually, we are a holy generation. A people holy to the Lord. He has chosen us out of all the other cultures (nations) of the earth to be His people, His treasured possession.

The Faithfulness of God

The Lord did not set his affection on you and choose you because you were more numerous than other peoples, for you were the fewest of all peoples. But it was because the Lord loved you and kept the oath he swore to your forefathers that he brought you out with a mighty hand and redeemed you from the land of slavery, from the power of Pharaoh king of Egypt. Know therefore that the Lord your God is God; he is the faithful God, keeping his covenant of love to a thousand generations of those who love him and keep his commands.

Deuteronomy 7:7-9

In the *King James Version* of Ephesians 3:20, the Apostle Paul tells us that God is able to do "exceeding abundantly" above anything we ask or think, according to the power, the ability, that is at work in us. The word *work* in that context refers to the force or vigor that is energized within us. So you and I, in cooperation with God, are able to do exploits — the impossible.

There is a great opposing worldly spirit now being exerted against the saints. But we have weapons that they (the spirits of this world) don't know about. The weapons of our warfare are not carnal, but mighty through God, empowered through God, energized through God, to the pulling down of strongholds, casting down every image and everything that tries to exalt itself above what we know about God or what we can identify and recognize about God. (2 Cor. 10:3-5.)

We serve a God Who is knowable. And to the God-hungry, searching heart, He is easy to recognize. He's easy to notice in His various creative expressions. I personally notice Him in weather, in a flower, in a sound, in a book, on the news, in a story, in a fragrance. He's everywhere. He even speaks to me experientially through things that I encounter. The Lord can speak to me through anything, because I look for Him in everything. I hear Him speaking in the news, in the weather report, in movies, and in magazine articles. In almost every circumstance of my life, I can hear the Holy Ghost speaking to me some precious spiritual parallel or lesson.

He speaks to me because I'm listening. He reveals Himself because I'm looking. I'm watching. I'm wanting God. He's not hard to find. He's easier to find than we are. We're the ones lost, not God. We were lost until He found us.

The Voice of God

Ask now about the former days, long before your time, from the day God created man on the earth; ask from one end of the heavens to the other. Has anything so great as this ever happened, or has anything like it ever been heard of? Has any other people heard the voice of God speaking out of fire, as you have, and lived?

Deuteronomy 4:32,33

The voice of God spoke to the children of Israel out of fire from the burning bush to the burning mountain to the burning bones of Jeremiah. He kept speaking to them down to the day of Pentecost, when cloven tongues like fire came and rested upon them and God addressed a nation through them. He spoke first to the spirit of the ones who received the gift — the eleven apostles and the others who were gathered there in the Upper Room. And to all those around, God spoke through flames of fire expressed in languages. In Old Testament fiery manifestations God was hinting about the baptism of the Holy Ghost to come.

"Have any other people heard the voice of God speaking out of fire as you have and lived?" asks Moses. "Has anybody been so close to God that His voice could be felt as well as heard?"

Today we feel the voice of God. His words are alive. They are Spirit and they are life. And when we have heard them, we have encountered God. We have been touched by divinity and with it. And we lived; that is prophetic fulfillment.

The Hand and Arm of God

> Has any god ever tried to take for himself one nation out of another nation, by testings, by miraculous signs and wonders, by war, by a *mighty hand* and an *outstretched arm,* or by great and awesome deeds, like all the things the Lord your God did for you in Egypt before your very eyes?
>
> Deuteronomy 4:34

Whenever you see the term "mighty hand," that's God's offensive tactics. And "an outstretched arm," that's defensive. By His mighty hand God offensively attacks our enemies, but with His arms He protects and defends us. We rest upon His everlasting arms. So God is both offensively and defensively providing for and protecting His chosen people.

God's Discipline

> You were shown these things so that you might know that the Lord is God; besides him there is no other. From heaven he made you hear his voice to discipline you....
>
> Deuteronomy 4:35,36

You and I are about to hear God's voice from heaven. No one else will know about it. God will speak to us directly and personally, and it will discipline and guide us. But when God disciplines us, we had better submit to His discipline, and we'd better honor His words.

The Presence of the Lord

> On earth he showed you his great fire, and you heard his words from out of the fire. Because he loved your forefathers and chose their descendants after them, he brought you out of Egypt by his Presence and his great strength, to drive out before you nations greater and stronger than you and to bring you into

78

**their land to give it to you for your inheritance, as it
is today.**

Deuteronomy 4:36-38

God brought us out of bondage to sin and death by
His presence. In His presence there is fullness of joy. (Ps.
16:11.) The word *presence* in this context means ''in His
face,'' or ''in His appearance.''

God appeared to the ancient Hebrews through outward
events. God's presence is about to manifest again, and it
will manifest in our generation just as it did then, by testings
and miraculous signs and wonders, by war, by a mighty
hand and an outstretched arm, by great and awesome
deeds.

Get ready for the presence of God to be manifested.
Look not only for the presence of God, but for the person
of Jesus to be made evident.

Because God loved our forefathers and chose their
descendants after them, He brought us out of our Egypt
by His presence and His great strength, to drive out before
us nations, cultures, greater and stronger than we are, and
to bring us into their land, to give it to us for our inheritance.

There are certain cultures and spirits that are active in
the earth today that are really stronger than you and I in
our natural strength. Only God can drive them out. But He
will not drive them out unless we enter in and take
possession of their lands.

There are no unoccupied territories. Every bit of land
we give up, the devil takes. So we must unseat him. We
must disinherit him by expulsion. We must drive out evil
spirits, demonic cultures. God has given us the anointing
to expel such cultures from our own marriages, from our
own homes, from our own families, from our own
businesses and churches. No weapon formed against us will
prosper.

You and I have a part to play in this mighty move of
God. The Lord is ready to give us carte blanche. Not because
we're so good, but because He is ready to get certain things

done in this hour. He's ready to kick up some dust. God is ready to reveal His power in the earth through the Church. He doesn't want to reveal it apart from the Body of Christ. He wants glory to be upon the Church, His body, the Body of Christ.

The Lord, He Is God

Acknowledge and take to heart this day that the Lord is God in heaven above and on the earth below. There is no other. Keep his decrees and commands, which I am giving you today, so that it may go well with you and your children after you and that you may live long in the land the Lord your God gives you for all time.

Deuteronomy 4:39,40

The Lord is saying here, "Look, take My authority which is delegated to you because of the intimacy you have with Me, and do what I'm asking you to do. It's not that hard. Just submit to Me. I am God. There is no other."

Do you realize Whom we serve and Whom we worship and from Whom we take our orders?

"Just recognize Who I am," says the Lord. "With the rights and authority and power and conviction that you have, no weapon formed against you will prosper. You can go into the land and overcome all of these other peoples and cultures. I will subdue them and you will cast them out of the land I am giving you. But do it completely. Don't even let them hang around the fringes. Drive them far from you."

I have never felt the energizing power of the Lord so strongly as I do at this moment. I believe that others are sensing it, too. The time has come to put God's plan and orders into action. Backed by His limitless power and authority, we are going to be able to say things by faith and see them happen before our very eyes because we're not going to say it unless God has placed it in our spirits. If we say that we are going to be blessed and prosperous, then we are going to be blessed and prosperous.

God is going to prosper us spiritually, mentally, physically, financially. The Lord is going to smile on us. He is going to make us glow. Our God is going to put us on display for the whole world to see because that is His sovereign will.

The Family of God

For this reason I kneel before the Father, from whom his whole family in heaven and on earth derives its name.

Ephesians 3:14,15

The Apostle Paul said that he knelt before the Father from Whom His whole family in heaven and on earth takes its name, its surname, its identity.

There is family in heaven and on earth. Not just those who have gone before us, but family members we have never met born of the same genetic background as you and I. One of these days we're going to have a great family reunion in heaven with those who bear the same name (and nature) as we do.

All the family in heaven and earth derives its name and its nature from Jesus.

Strengthened With God's Power

I pray that out of his glorious riches he may strengthen you with power through his Spirit in your inner being, so that Christ may dwell in your hearts through faith....

Ephesians 3:16,17

It is Paul's prayer that out of God's apparent abundance He might strengthen us with power, with supernatural ability, through His Spirit Who resides in our inner being so that Christ might dwell in our hearts by faith. With God's riches, ability and presence in us, could there possibly be anything too difficult for us to accomplish for the Lord?

The Theme of Love

...And I pray that you, being rooted and established in love, may have power, together with all the saints, to grasp how wide and long and high and deep is the love of Christ, and to know this love that surpasses knowledge — that you may be filled to the measure of all the fullness of God.

Ephesians 3:17-19

What Paul is praying for us here is that we might be established and stabilized in the love of God which runs through us.

Love should be the theme and topic of our lives. The woven thematic of God in any Christian is love. **"All men will know that you are my disciples,"** said Jesus, **"if you love one another"** (John 13:35). He also commanded us, **"...let your light** [your love] **shine before men, that they may see your good deeds** [works of love] **and praise your Father in heaven"** (Matt. 5:16).

In this passage from Ephesians, when Paul speaks of love, the Greek word he uses is *agape* which means "benevolence" or "affection." His prayer for us is that we may have power and ability, together with all the saints, to grasp how wide and long and high and deep is God's benevolence and affection toward us. Only by the Spirit can we grasp it. It is a supernatural task. It is impossible by the flesh. But God wants to reveal to us the depth and height and width of His love.

We are about to experience that depth of love, that depth of intimacy. We are going higher and deeper in the love of God. The glory of the Lord is about to fall upon us. We're crossing over.

If you will get this truth in your spirit, there will be a new command in your soul. A new confidence. You will begin to grasp how wide and long and high and deep is the love of Christ, and will begin to know, to identify, to recognize, this love that surpasses all human knowledge.

As a result, you will be filled to the measure of the fullness of God.

I want you to literalize this passage. Let God fill you with the measure of His fullness. Just get so full of God that if you are put in a squeeze, nothing but Jesus comes out. If the pressure is on you, the juice of joy just flows from you.

As someone has said, ''We should be so full of the Lord that if a mosquito bites us he'll fly off singing 'There's power in the blood!''' You should be just exuding with God, just sticky with love. When you walk into a room, the entire spiritual aroma of that room should change.

Have you noticed that when you drive by a donut place you can usually smell the pastry? There's a reason for that. It's to entice you into the shop to make a purchase. Kentucky Fried Chicken has a way of sending the fragrance of its food out on the street to draw in hungry customers.

In the same way, there is a fragrance that comes with holiness, and it's very attractive and alluring. It's the glory of the Lord, and it is on you and me.

God's Immeasurable Power

Now to him who is able to do immeasurably more than all we ask or imagine, according to his power that is at work within us, to him be glory in the church and in Christ Jesus throughout all generations, for ever and ever! Amen.

Ephesians 3:20,21

God's power cannot be measured. He is able to do ''immeasurably more.'' He is going to move us into His measureless ''more.'' Are you ready to enter into the more of God? The more of His love? The more of His blessing? Are you ready for there to be more of God and less of you?

The glory of the Lord is on its way. The more of God is coming. When I say ''the more,'' I mean ''the muchness'' and ''the allness'' and ''the everywhere'' of Him.

The Lord is able to do immeasurably more than we ask. In Greek, that word translated *ask* means ''to beg,'' ''to call for,'' or ''to crave.'' God is able to do more than we are able to ask for or even desire. More than we are able to require. He's able to do more than we can even feel.

I am asking, and I am thinking. I am imagining. I have a spiritual image in my mind. I have the power, the ability, to realize what I imagine and to receive what I ask. That power is at work in me every day.

You have the same power. It is already at work in you. Together we cannot fail.

To God be glory in the Church and in Christ Jesus throughout all generations for ever and ever! Amen.

6
God's Midwives

Jeremiah was one of Israel's greatest and most commanding prophets. He happens to be both my favorite and least favorite prophet.

He is my least favorite prophet in that he prophesied for almost seventy years, forty years actively, and all of that time he prophesied doom and destruction rather than salvation and faith. Not only did he prophesy doom, but he had to live through it.

If I'm going to prophesy doom, I want to prophesy it and then die and go to heaven. But Jeremiah prophesied some rather unpleasant things, and then lived through the fulfillment of his prophesy. All the time he was prophesying he was saying to the people, "If you repent, these prophecies will never be fulfilled." He preached salvation and faith, but he prophesied death and destruction.

Isaiah had prophesied two hundred years earlier, with some measure of success, against the Assyrian insurgents, and the nation had repented. As a result, Assyria was defeated as an empire. Then Babylon followed Assyria because the people of God had gotten into idolatry and come under judgment for disobedience. Now Jeremiah has risen to take the place of Isaiah, God's spokesman.

Jeremiah was a commanding figure. He was lonely and pathetic, but he was still an incredibly resolute, resilient, and courageously obedient servant of God. He is called the weeping prophet. In addition to the book of Jeremiah, he wrote the book of Lamentations, which means literally "to beat the breast."

Jeremiah lamented, he wept and beat upon his breast, because he saw a cloud of destruction coming upon his people — and he didn't see any hope of success at turning it back.

In our day, I see a cloud of destruction on the horizon. But it is not only coming, it's already over the land. The difference is that I feel the faith of God to turn it back. I believe we can turn storm clouds into the latter rain of the outpouring of the Holy Spirit in our generation. I've got a feelin' everything's gonna be all right.

The Gathering Storm

When Jeremiah was exercising his prophetic ministry, it was during a time much like today, a period of reoccurring crisis. One dilemma after another. Rapid change. Uncertainty of the future.

Recently we heard that another former Congressman, Sen. John Towers, was killed in an accident. About the same time, an astronaut was killed. Soon afterwards, Senator Hines from Pennsylvania was killed in a plane crash. Whenever national news emphasizes something, it's generally a sign in the natural of what may happen in the spiritual.

Watch, there's going to be a shaking and a shifting. Some people will be taken from us suddenly, tragically, prematurely. They will be recognized entities. There is a changing of the guards in the leadership of the Church. Things are going to look bad for a while. Like Jeremiah, I'm warning you now that these things will happen. And every time I have ever spoken the prophetic message the Lord has given me, it has come to pass. I only speak it as God shows me. He told me that the world is on automatic pilot, and it's headed for danger. However, the Church is not on cruise control. There are dangers at numerous times for us all. We need God's personal involvement and divine intervention.

You don't put an airplane on automatic pilot when you're going through tumultuous weather. You've got to have the pilot and navigator in command of the craft. Let me tell you Who that pilot and navigator is. It is Jesus Christ, the Son of the Living God.

God is in charge of our future, our destiny, and He told me to crawl up into the lap of His sovereignty and rest a while. He's about to do something. There is going to be some rough weather through which this ship must travel, but God is at the controls.

The Weeping Prophet

Jeremiah was not, as far as we know, successful at anything he attempted. He was somewhat like Noah, who preached 120 years and ended up saving no one but his wife and children. Sometimes God puts something on a preacher that is very unpleasant to deal with. But the reason Jeremiah could carry on his ministry was because he was dedicated to the Lord and convinced of the truth of His Word. The people he loved so much and served so long didn't want to hear his message.

And yet the Bible calls Jeremiah a fortified city, a bronze pillar, an iron wall. He was criticized and conspired against. He was considered a traitor and often put in prison. He was called the weeping prophet because he had high highs and low lows.

But through it all, he never aborted his vision, the prophetic "baby" which he carried in the "womb" of his spirit. I believe Jeremiah continued, despite the hardship, rejection, persecution and failure, because he carried something in his spirit that had been planted there by God. The egg of his faith had been fertilized by the seed of God. And he carried that "fetus" through to full term.

I am pregnant with a vision from the Lord. And whether you know it or not, so are you. I would venture to say that every Christian is pregnant with a vision, with a dream, with a miracle. Every minister is pregnant, every child of God has the seed of the Lord in him or her — and something is about to come forth.

Pregnant Faith

O my Comforter in sorrow, my heart is faint within me.

Jeremiah 8:18

This is the lament of Jeremiah, the weeping prophet. The *King James Version* of this verse reads, **When I would comfort myself against sorrow, my heart is faint in me.** The Hebrew word translated *sorrow* here is *yagown* meaning "grief" or "affliction."

"When I would comfort myself in affliction or grief or sorrow, my heart (my emotions, my will) is faint within me."

In Hebrew the word translated *faint* in this passage means "sick" or "troubled." It's the same word that is used in reference to a woman in menstrual pain. Menstruation is a monthly sign of fertility.

So here is a man using the same term. He is saying, "My heart is fertile. My heart is repeatedly reminding me that the spirit of fertility is in my soul."

The Cry of the People

Listen to the cry of my people from a land far away:

"Is the Lord not in Zion? Is her King no longer there?"

"Why have they provoked me to anger with their images, with their worthless foreign idols?"

Jeremiah 8:19

At the time Jeremiah wrote these words, most of the people of Judah were in captivity in faraway Babylon.

Today our people are in exile. They are away from God. Many Christians are backslidden. As I look about me at the current state of our nation, I cry out, "God, look at the people. They're so far away from You."

Look at the shape of America today with its crime-ridden, drug-infested neighborhoods. When I go back home to San Diego where I was born and reared, I hardly know the place. There are gangs on the street and wrought-iron bars on all the windows of the businesses and houses. Many parents are frightened by their own children, whom they don't even know. I'm cautious even to walk down the street. I don't feel at home anymore.

Some of those kids who are growing up on the streets look like little animals in the face. Their eyes are hollow and empty. I keep thinking, "My God, I need to cast the devil out of this whole neighborhood."

Listen to the cry of my people in a land far away:

"Is the Lord not in Zion? Is her King no longer there?"....

Jeremiah 8:19

In other words, the prophet inquires: "Has the Lord left home? Has He changed addresses? Is He no longer there?"

We Are Not Saved

"The harvest is past, the summer has ended, and we are not saved."

Jeremiah 8:20

The prophet is crying out in distress, "The time of harvest is over, and we're still not saved. Still not free. Still not delivered. Still not rescued from the impending destruction."

We in the Church are still not completely delivered ourselves. We're still fussing and feuding and fighting and cursing one another. We're still divided. But God is going to change that situation. And if anyone or anything tries to hinder Him, the Lord will move that person or thing out of the way. Our generation is not accustomed to the kinds of things which occurred in the past that divided God's Church and destroyed its unity, power, and effectiveness.

I want a move of God. How about you? I'm tired of the games people play — including ministers.

One of the things I've had to face as a black clergyman is the fact that black people in general don't have respect for the minister anymore. They think all preachers are skirt-chasers or money-grabbers. Some of them have seen so much of that kind of thing going on, they don't know how to believe anything else. But God told me to raise the integrity of the preacher in our community and bring the Church back into proper relationship with its community through the Lord Jesus Christ.

My People Are Crushed

Since my people are crushed, I am crushed; I mourn, and horror grips me.

Jeremiah 8:21

What the prophet is saying is: "Since my people are hurt or broken or injured or crippled, so am I." The *King James Version* of this verse says, **For the hurt of the daughter of my people am I hurt; I am black....** He is not talking about his color, he is saying, "I am dressed in black," or, "I am in mourning; I am bereaved because death is all around us."

We Christians meet in our churches and shout and rejoice, having a wonderful time in the Lord. I am glad that we do that. But my mind has come to dwell on the people who aren't in church anywhere. Not those who are in another church, but those who aren't in anybody's church. Those who are stumbling up and down the streets in cities and towns all across our nation, oblivious to God and numb to the moving of His Spirit.

I have a friend who is an associate minister of a church and a member of the Los Angeles Police Department. He has told me some incredible stories about his work. Did you know there are over nine hundred homicides in Los Angeles each year? There were ninety-eight in this man's precinct alone.

He remembers seeing two young men, one twenty and the other twenty-one. One had been shot in the mouth and

90

neck, the other shot in the head. They were lying on the street with their blood oozing out of their bodies. It started raining and the rainwater washed their blood into the sewer. Those boys lay there in the rain for three and a half hours. Our police officers go through tremendous stress. They need our prayers — they need our God.

There was an article in the newspaper about this same friend with a photograph of him praying. He holds a Bible in one hand and a pistol in the other. That is a good picture of the state of our nation at this point in history.

But I predict and prophesy in the name of the Lord that things are about to change. I'm going to be a part of that change. How about you?

Is There No Balm in Gilead?

Is there no balm in Gilead? Is there no physician there? Why then is there no healing for the wound of my people?

Jeremiah 8:22

When the prophet asks, "Is there no balm in Gilead?" he is being facetious. He actually says, "Isn't there a balm in Gilead?" The inference here is, yes, there is. The word *balm* really means "a healing salve" or "medication."

Gilead was a city in the Middle East known for its medical scientists, hospitals, and clinics. People from all over the ancient world came to that city just as they go to the Mayo Clinic here in the United States.

"Is there no physician there?" the prophet asks rhetorically. In the original Hebrew the word translated *physician* suggests to mend by stitching. "Isn't there anybody there to stitch up the wound [or in some cases, the womb] of my people?" asks Jeremiah.

Is God in heaven? Can't He deliver His people from their distress? Can't He save anybody? Can't He heal anyone?

91

In most cities of this country, we can ride down the street and see a church on every corner. They are of all different sizes, shapes, names, and affiliations. Sometimes we can find two, three, or four right next door to each other. And yet the newspapers report that the violent crime rate is increasing. Drug use is rising. What is happening? Is there no balm in Gilead?

That's the cry of a preacher's heart asking, "God, are You there? I feel You in my private times, I feel You on Sunday morning, but I need to feel You when I'm walking down the street. I need to feel and see You in my country and in our land."

I can't be satisfied. Some people think that we are successful because they see us on television all over the country. We're building new churches and growing. But I'm not satisfied with that alone. I'm not unthankful, but I know that we are not doing even a fraction of what we're supposed to be doing or what we could be doing for the Lord.

Instead of carrying forth the great revival that is needed, we in the Church have become involved in civil rights movements, philanthropy, and sectarianism. We have gotten so caught up in all kinds of outward activity, we have lost the anointing and power of the Lord. We need to stop fighting the problem and start applying the solution.

I'm declaring war on the devil. I'm angry with Satan and his demons. I'm tired of running from devils. Devils ought to be running from us. The Bible says that greater is He Who is in us than he who is in the world. (1 John 4:4.) We have the power to overthrow Satan's kingdom and reclaim our nation and world for the Lord. And no weapon formed against us will prosper.

Is there no balm? Is there no healing? Is there no physician? Can God do it? Can *we* do it?

Yes, we're going to change things. The government can't do it, the police officers can't do it, the penal institutions can't do it. The Church has got to rise up and be God's people and accomplish His will on earth.

"Why then is there no healing for the wound of the daughter of my people?" asks the weeping prophet. The Hebrew word translated *daughter* in this verse comes from a root word which signifies the ability to obtain offspring, children.

Is there no health, no wholeness, no well-being for the spirit of offspring? Why is there such barrenness in the land? Why are there so many closed-up wombs? Why is there so much spiritual infertility?

Statistics indicate that the United States has the highest infant mortality rate per capita of any country in the western hemisphere. It's not because we don't have good doctors, obstetricians, gynecologists, and pediatricians. It's because we have the worst pre-natal care of any civilized nation. We do not know how to take care of our pregnant citizens.

When a woman gets pregnant, she has to eat differently, exercise differently, think differently, and act differently.

Let me tell you something prophetically. The Church is pregnant with revival, and the revival is already in the birth canal. But it is in the same situation described in Isaiah 37:3: "...**This day is a day of distress and rebuke and disgrace, as when children come to the point of birth and there is no strength to deliver them.**" Today in the Church of Jesus Christ, there is no substance, no ability, no capacity to deliver. The daughter of God's people is pregnant, but too weak to bring forth the baby.

I've been told that some pregnant women feel unattractive and stretched and heavy and ugly. They are miserable and even begin to think their husbands don't love them anymore. They may have terrible mood swings at times. There's a hormonal change in their bodies. Their hormones go wild, and many begin to crave weird foods at all hours or are repelled by the smell of what was their favorite food before. Some get moody and sensitive.

Sometimes they don't want to be around their husbands and don't want to talk to anybody.

A healthy pregnant woman is one of the most beautiful creatures you'll ever see in your life. Everything in her body is alerted to take care of that little baby. Her eyes are radiant, her cheeks are rosy, her skin is clear, her hair is shiny and rich. She looks like a different human being. She may feel unattractive. She may feel overweight and heavy. She may have lower back pain. But if she wasn't willing to go through all that, she would never produce a child.

Spiritually you may feel ugly and heavy and stretched. You may not feel like taking in much spiritual food. You may be moody and sensitive, unable to find rest and contentment. It could be because you are pregnant — pregnant with a vision from the Lord. The symptoms are par for the course, but the victory lies ahead.

Weeping, Travailing Prophets

Oh, that my head were a spring of water and my eyes a fountain of tears! I would weep day and night for the slain of my people.

Jeremiah 9:1

We need more weeping prophets who can feel the intensity and burden, travailing prophets who will cry and walk the floor in prayer and intercession.

Sometimes I get up in the middle of the night and pace back and forth praying: "Lord, You've got to do something about this situation we are in. What's the matter, Father? Why don't You do something to save Your people? What can I do, Lord? What should I do?"

Have you ever prayed until you thought you were losing your mind? I have actually lain face down on the floor and cried out, "Oh, God, I think I'm going crazy. Something is coming up out of me, and I don't know what it is."

"You're travailing," said the Lord. "You're in labor. You are about to give birth to something. Don't stop

94

praying. Don't abort that vision, and don't miscarry it. The devil didn't give it to you, I did. Don't let the enemy take it away from you.''

Oh, for a Place of Rest

Oh, that I had in the desert a lodging place for travelers, so that I might leave my people and go away from them; for they are all adulterers, a crowd of unfaithful people.

Jeremiah 9:2

A lot of preachers (prophets) are honest enough to admit that, as much as they love the Church and the Lord, there are times when they feel like praying, ''O God, let me get away from these people. I've got to get out of here.''

You remember the biblical account of Moses being on the mountaintop, bathed in God's glory, and receiving the Ten Commandments. It was a glorious time that lasted for forty days and nights. But then suddenly the Lord ordered Moses to get back down the mountain because the children of Israel were engaging in sin and rebellion.

I'm sure Moses must have been thinking, ''Lord, I don't want to go down where the people are. I want to stay on the mountaintop with You.''

There are a lot of preachers who say, ''Lord, I don't want to go down there.'' But the Lord says to them, ''Get down there and pay your bills. Get down there and take care of your community, your marriage, your life. Get down there and tend to My business.''

The story is told of a mother who went into the bedroom of her son one Sunday morning and said, ''Son, get out of that bed and get on down to the church. You're going to be late.''

He didn't budge. She came in the second time. ''Son, get out of that bed and get on down to the church. You're going to be late.''

He still didn't move. She came the third time. She shook the bed, pulled back the blanket, and said, ''Boy, get out of that bed and get on down to the church. You're going to be late.''

He looked up at her and said, ''Mother, I'll give you two reasons why I'm not going. First, there are people down there who do not like me. And second, there are people down there I do not like.''

The mother said, ''Boy, I'm going to give you two reasons why you've got to get out of that bed and get down there to that church. First, you're forty-seven years old. And second, you are the pastor of the church.''

I don't have that problem. I am so full in the Spirit, I have to be faithful in service to my church. I have no choice, because I am pregnant with a vision from the Lord. I must carry it through to full term.

Women Experienced in Travail

This is what the Lord Almighty says: ''Consider now! Call for the wailing women to come; send for the most skillful of them.

''Let them come quickly and wail over us....''
Jeremiah 9:17,18

This passage recalls the Lord's words to Israel as recorded in Isaiah 66:9. **''Do I bring to the moment of birth and not give delivery?'' says the Lord. ''Do I close up the womb when I bring to delivery?'' says your God.**

God is going to bring His people to full term and delivery.

''Send for the most skillful, or cunning, or knowledgeable, or spiritual, or experienced women,'' says the Lord to Jeremiah. ''Let them wail over you.'' The word *wail* means ''to chant, lament, groan or travail.''

The Lord is saying, ''Find some women who know how to give birth to spiritual babies. Women who know how to groan and travail and lament until the infant comes forth.''

Our God is telling us to find somebody, man or woman, who has the spirit of fertility and knows how to walk the floor until the miracle comes. Somebody who won't take no for an answer, someone to help bring forth the vision.

The Bible says that the Kingdom of God suffers violence, and the violent take it by force. (Matt. 11:12.) Take it by force. You've got the power. You've got the authority. You've got the blessing. Take the Kingdom by force. Get some experienced ones, those who know how to cast out the devil. Those who know how to walk the floor until that boy is saved. Those who know how to hold on until that marriage is changed. **"Let them come quickly and wail over us till our eyes overflow with tears and water streams from our eyelids"** (Jer. 9:18), until we bring forth that which the Lord has planted within us.

The Sound of Wailing

The sound of wailing is heard from Zion: "How ruined we are! How great is our shame! We must leave our land because our houses are in ruins."

Jeremiah 9:19

I believe God is going to pull back the curtain, and the spirit of prosperity is going to come on the Church. On God's people. While the banking institutions are crumbling, God's Church is going to rise like an island in the sea. But in order for that to happen, there must be a period of labor, just as when a woman gives birth to a child.

The Lord tells us to call for the women who know how to pray, those who know how to groan, travail, and intercede.

Where are the wailing women? Where are the weeping widows? Where are the spiritual midwives who help to bring forth new birth, new life, in our churches?

In Romans 8:26,27 we are told by the Apostle Paul: **In the same way, the Spirit helps us in our weakness. We do not know what we ought to pray for, but the Spirit himself intercedes for us with groans that words cannot express. And he who searches our hearts knows the mind of the**

Spirit, because the Spirit intercedes for the saints in accordance with God's will.

The Holy Spirit intercedes for us. That means that He acts as a go-between. He negotiates with God. He barters on our behalf. He prays through us with groans and travail, bringing forth from us that which God has planted within us.

Should we in the Church not do as much for others? Should we not groan, weep, wail, lament, travail, and labor until we have brought forth in the Church God's perfect will and plan for His people throughout the world?

7

Destiny: God's
Determination for Your Life

This is the time for the Church of Jesus Christ to do exploits for God. I don't believe that anything is going to stop us because we are coming into a new era of God's times and seasons. You should believe that about yourself and about the Church. When an individual really believes in what he is doing, the mission to which he has been called of God, no weapon formed against him can prosper.

You must have firm belief in the Word and will of God as you understand it. You must be convinced of your divine destiny, God's determination for your life.

According to Webster's dictionary, the English word *determination* is a derivative of the Latin *de terminare* meaning "to limit." The noun form is the equivalent of termination, the end, the conclusion. Thus, there is a settled conclusiveness about God.

With God, there is a final resolve, and it's not an illusionary thing. There is a definite *modus operandi.* There is a master plan of hope of which we are a part. This spiritual warfare in which we are engaged is a fixed fight. There is a termination to it, and at the conclusion of it all, we are going to be declared the winners!

Solomon said, **Trust in the Lord with all your heart and lean not on your own understanding; in all your ways acknowledge him** [identify Him, recognize Him], **and he will make your paths straight** (Prov. 3:5,6).

I strongly believe that as a people, as a Church, we are in the precise center of the will of God. I even believe that I am there myself. God has some bounds and limits and endings for me. I don't know exactly what they are just yet, but I'm resting in the knowledge that as I follow Him in faithful obedience, He will direct my paths and make them straight.

The Lord is a sovereign God. He spoke to me some time ago and said, "Crawl up in the lap of sovereignty and rest a while." I don't worry or fret or become anxious or discouraged. I'm too busy to be worried; I'm too busy to be discouraged because discouragement is a waste of time. It has no meaningful or significant value.

You and I should lay aside every doubt, fear, and worry, and press on, keeping up our faith, courage, and determination because there is an end to all of our world encounters and, in that end, we emerge victorious. I've already looked at the end of the book. The devil has won some battles, but he won't win the war. As I heard a basketball coach once say, "I'd rather fail at something that will ultimately succeed than to succeed at something that will ultimately fail." We are not going to fail. Destiny is God's determination for us.

Present Suffering, Future Glory

I consider that our present sufferings are not worth comparing with the glory that will be revealed in us.
Romans 8:18

The Greek word translated *sufferings* in this verse refers to something which must be put up with, endured, or withstood. So the full implication of what the Apostle Paul was writing here is: "I consider that our present withstandings, our present waitings and wantings and wrestlings, our current fightings and battles, are not worthy to be compared with the glory, the clarity, the obviousness, that will be revealed in us."

I don't mind suffering if I can just have a little clarity. I just want to know why I'm suffering. I want to know the clear objective. Paul tells us that what we must suffer for a limited time has no comparison with the clarity, the dignity, the praise and light that will be revealed, disclosed, uncovered in us both during and after the suffering.

100

Creation Waits for Revelation

The creation waits in eager expectation for the sons of God to be revealed.

Romans 8:19

The whole earth is groaning and waiting for the sons of God, the offspring of God, to be uncovered, revealed, disclosed, unveiled.

The Coming Liberation

For the creation was subjected to frustration, not by its own choice, but by the will of the one who subjected it, in hope, that the creation itself will be liberated from its bondage to decay and brought into the glorious freedom of the children of God.

Romans 8:20,21

When Adam sinned, God said to him, ''Cursed is the ground because of you.'' (Gen. 3:17.) So all of the ground, the earth, has been groaning under a curse, waiting for God's people to be revealed in glory so that it can receive the same freedom as they.

Something is going to happen to this planet. This whole terrestrial ball is going to change at the second coming of the Lord. The Bible says there will be a new heaven and a new earth. (Rev. 21:1.) There is a good ending.

Regardless of what happens on this earth right now, there is still a positive ending, a new heaven and a new earth.

Waiting Eagerly

We know that the whole creation has been groaning as in the pains [or travail or pangs] of childbirth right up to the present time. Not only so, but we ourselves, who have the firstfruits of the Spirit, groan [sigh] inwardly as we wait eagerly for our adoption as sons, the redemption of our bodies.

Romans 8:22,23

The expression *wait eagerly* means "to expect fully" with strained expectation, with eager longing, with abstraction from anything else that might engage the attention.

We believers, we who have the firstfruits of the Spirit of God, groan as in labor or travail, waiting with eager anticipation for our adoption as sons, for the redemption of our physical bodies.

In Hope

For in this hope we were saved. But hope that is seen is no hope at all. Who hopes for what he already has? But if we hope for what we do not yet have, we wait for it patiently.

Romans 8:24,25

The word *hope* in Greek is *elpis* which means "happy anticipation of good." Paul says that it is in this happy anticipation of a good ending that we were saved.

If there was going to be a bad ending to this struggle, I don't know if I'd even think about salvation. If I didn't believe this thing was going to end right and that we were going to win, I'd give up on the battle. But because I already know that we win, that it is a fixed fight, I continue the struggle in happy anticipation. There is a divine destiny, a successful determination, to which I aspire.

The Spirit Intercedes

In the same way, the Spirit helps us in our weakness. We do not know what we ought to pray, but the Spirit himself intercedes for us with groans that words cannot express.

Romans 8:26

Sometimes I get so confused because intellectually I don't know specifically what to ask for — especially in regard to a wife. I don't want to ask according to my own desires or ideas, because I might ask in my flesh and get the wrong thing. The writer of Proverbs says, **He who finds a wife**

finds what is good and receives favor from the Lord (Prov. 18:22). This verse really means that he that runs across her in his traveling. . . . It doesn't mean that he's out there searching for her. I'm waiting to accidentally, incidently, stumble across my future bride.

By nature I'm too objective. I've got a list of requirements. I know exactly the size, shape, measurements, shoe size, and financial status of the woman I am looking for as a mate. I've got it all written down. But I don't trust my own objectiveness. Instead I have to say, ''Lord, I don't know what to ask for, because what I'm asking for may not be at all what You have in mind for me.'' So what I'm going to do at almost forty years of age is crawl up in His lap and rest. God already has a plan, and I believe I am in it.

I believe that I am flowing down the right channel and that everything that is supposed to be allotted to Carlton Pearson will come. That which is not allotted the hand cannot reach, and that which is allotted will be found whatever the location.

It's coming. The end is right and good. The Holy Ghost knows our inability to make proper decisions or choices, so He helps us. He intervenes, He intercedes (sometimes He even interferes or interrupts to prevent unscheduled detours), He sustains us and assists us, for we don't even know what to pray for as we ought.

You may be praying for wrong things in the name of Jesus. You can pray for the wrong thing and get it. You can end up with an Ishmael rather than an Isaac. The problem with Ishmaels is that you can't kill them because they're part God. They came out of the same promise. So once you get an Ishmael you may lose Isaac. Once you receive what you asked for, you may wish you had let God choose for you.

That's why it is to our advantage to allow the Holy Spirit to help us in our prayers. We don't always know what we ought to pray for, but the Holy Ghost does. He intercedes for us. He acts as a go-between. We pray, he intercedes. He stands in the way and clears a passage for our prayer.

He intervenes, intercedes for us with groans and sighs and pains that words cannot express, that baffles speech.

According to the Will of God

And he who searches our hearts knows the mind of the Spirit, because the Spirit intercedes for the saints in accordance with God's will.

Romans 8:27

The Holy Spirit intercedes, investigates, or identifies. He sees, He recognizes by observation, the intentions of our heart. He then intercedes for us in accordance with the will of God.

The Holy Ghost stands there intervening, allowing the things to go through that are in the will of God. If something is not in the will of God, He blocks it. He can intercede, or He can interfere for those who want the will of God.

If you don't want the will of God, you don't have to depend on the Holy Ghost. Just do your own thing. But when you're praying in the Holy Ghost, the Spirit steps in and intercedes or interferes according to the will of God for you in that situation.

God has everything under control. We are in the will of God. And when we are flowing in that divine place, no weapon formed against us can prosper. Nothing can hinder, obstruct, obscure, or bind us.

I feel like I can run through a troop. I can leap over walls. (Ps. 18:29.) My time has come. Our time has come. We are children of destiny.

God Works for Our Good

And we know that in all things God works for the good of those who love him, who have been called according to his purpose.

Romans 8:28

The *King James Version* of this scripture is probably more familiar to most believers: **And we know that all things work together for good to them that love God, to them who are the called according to his purpose.** The Greek word translated *work together* in this version is *sunergeo*, meaning "energize together," "cooperate," "collaborate," or "coincide."

A school teacher took a group of ingredients — flour, eggs, baking powder, milk, vanilla, sugar, chocolate — and let her students taste them individually. As they tasted each raw ingredient, the pupils either said "Yuck!" or "Mmmm!" When they had finished tasting, they did a count and discovered that there were more "Yucks!" than "Mmmms!" But when the teacher mixed all the ingredients together and baked them in the oven, it came out a chocolate cake. When the pupils tasted the final product, they all agreed — "Mmmm!"

That's the way God works with the events and circumstances of our lives. He takes the individual "ingredients," mixes them together in the "oven" of time, and eventually brings forth something good.

All the ingredients of life, the bitter and the sweet, the good and the bad, are working together for our well-being, for our ultimate benefit. For the good of those of us who love God.

In the original Greek, this word *love* is *agapao* meaning "to love (in a social or moral sense)." It is the verb form of *agape* which is defined as "affection" or "benevolence." All things work together for good for those who have a benevolent, social affection for God, for those who are called of God.

105

In this context the word *called* means "invited." In all things God works for the good of those who love Him, those who have been called, invited, according to His purpose, His plan, His divine destiny.

You and I are among those who love God. We are called according to His express purpose and design. What God does, He does intentionally. He is not an accidental God. He knows exactly what He's doing. And since you and I are the specifically, intentionally called of God, nothing that comes against us can ultimately overcome or defeat us.

The Bible says, **No temptation has seized you except what is common to man. And God is faithful; he will not let you be tempted** [taxed or tried] **beyond what you can bear. But when you are tempted, he will also provide a way out so that you can stand up under it** (1 Cor. 10:13).

Temptations, tests, trials, and tribulations will come to us. They seem to be part of the ingredients of life. But God has promised to provide a way for us to handle them so we can stand up under them.

Therefore, we know that, whatever comes our way in life, God is working it all together for our good, for the eventual fulfillment of our divine destiny.

Predestined by God

For those God foreknew he also predestined to be conformed to the likeness of his Son, that he might be the firstborn among many brothers.

Romans 8:29

To foreknow is to know beforehand, to foresee. The Hebrew word meaning "to know" is *yada*, from which I think the writers took the name Yoda for the wise old character in the Star Wars trilogy. It means "to ascertain by seeing," "observation," "care," "recognition."

The Bible says that Jesus Christ is the Lamb of God that was slain before the foundation of the world. (Rev. 13:8.) That means that God had already planned salvation long before man ever sinned. The Lord knew what man would do. So before the fall of man ever took place, God had already provided a plan for his redemption. And you and I are included in that plan.

God foreknew us. Not in the sense of reincarnation in another life in which we were a fly or a mosquito or a moth or some Egyptian prince or princess. God knew us because He created us. He knew us when we were still just an embryo. When the egg had been fertilized by the sperm. The Bible says that we cannot sin because God's seed remains in us. (1 John 3:9.) The Lord knew us when the egg of our faith was fertilized by the seed of God, when we were still in our mother's womb. David said, "When I was still in my mother's womb, all the days ordained for me were written in a book." (Ps. 139:13,15,16.)

You and I are no accident. God planned for us to be here. God has us here for a reason. There is a plan for our life. And the Lord plans for us to win and not lose. He plans for us to be the head and not the tail, the first and not the last, to be victorious. In the end, we win.

God foreknew that we would become His children. So those whom He foreknew He also predestined. The dictionary defines the word *destiny* as "the inevitable or necessary succession of events; what will necessarily or eminently happen to one, regardless."

Destiny is one's future, or one's fortune in one sense. It is that which determines events or eventualities. Our destiny has been predetermined by God. We are a destined people.

The word *destined* comes from two Latin words meaning "to stand." It refers to something that is predetermined by fate — or in our case, by faith. Our destiny is predetermined, ordained by divine decree. We stand affirmed in and by God from the beginning. Because He foreknew us, He put us in our proper place and set boundaries around us.

Those God foreknew He predestined. In Greek the word *predestined* is *proorizo,* which is derived from two root words meaning "to limit in advance," "to predetermine, preordain, or preorder," "to mark out boundaries." This not only determines where we can go, but where we cannot go. Our future is marked out by boundaries. Nothing can stop us or hinder us from reaching our destination, because we are engaged in a preordained, prearranged process.

God has predestined us. He has prearranged for our success. He knew us when He created us, and He made a preordained plan for our success.

Those whom God foreknew He predestined to be conformed to the likeness of His Son. The Greek word translated *conformed* in Romans 8:29 is *summorphos*, which is itself a combination of two Greek words: *sun*, denoting union, and *morphe* meaning "shape, "nature," or "form." (The word *metamorphosis* means "change of form.") Thus, *summorphos* means "formed in union," "jointly fashioned" or "attached together." It refers to the fastening of our form to that of God's Son.

Because God foreknew us, He predestined us to be attached in form genetically to His Son, Jesus Christ — to be born of His Spirit. The word *born* in Greek is *gennao*, which is where we get the English word *genetics*. When we are reborn, we are really *regenerated*. We have a new *gene* within us, and we become a new *generation* with a new *genealogy*.

As the children of God, our genes have been changed. When we were reborn, we were regenerated, actually joined to God. We became a part of the hand of God, a part of the arm of God, a part of the body of God.

Everything's Gonna Be All Right!

And those he predestined, he also called; those he called, he also justified; those he justified, he also glorified.

What, then, shall we say in response to this? If God is for us, who can be against us?

Romans 8:30,31

If God is for us, who (or what) can be against us? There's no stopping us now.

Jesus said, "Upon this rock I will build My Church, and the gates of hell will not prevail against it." (Matt. 16:18.) That means that the gates of hell cannot withstand the violent onslaught of holy people who know who they are and who do exploits for their God.

As I stated earlier, the devil has won a few battles, but he won't win the war. You and I are a threat to the enemy. We are joined to God. We are private property. We are part of His body. He has predestined us to be conformed to His image, His likeness.

In Greek that word translated *image* is *eikon*. It means "a resemblance," "a representation." You and I are a living profile of Jesus. We are a resemblance, an icon of Jesus, not made of gold or metal, but by the Holy Ghost. Everywhere we go, we resemble Jesus — and demons know that. But they cannot stop us from fulfilling our God-ordained destiny.

Our God predestined us to be conformed to the likeness of His Son, that He (Jesus) might be the firstborn among many brothers. Jesus is our brother, our elder brother. He is the firstborn, the eldest in the family.

And those God predestined, preordained, or preordered, He also called. The Greek word translated *called* is *kaleo*, meaning "to bid, call forth, call by (sur)name." Those God predestined, He bid, called forth, called by name. He gave birth to them. Once God foreknows us, and predestines us, and calls us, then He actually forms us, births us, and gives us a surname.

Our last name is of God. Our given name is our particular vocation, but our last name suggests our nature. It bespeaks our character. Even if a person is adopted, he takes on the name of his father. And we are adopted into the family of God. When you take on somebody's name, you take on his benefits. You become an heir to his fortune and his future.

So what the Lord is saying to us here is: "I have called you forth, and I have given you a last name. And that last name is known and recognized by demons. It lets them know Who you belong to. It identifies your family line."

You and I are wrapped up, tied up, tangled up, in Jesus. In Him we live and move and have our being. (Acts 17:28.)

Those God predestined He also called, and those He called He justified. To be justified is to be set in right standing, in right position, in right posture, in right relationship with God. The Lord has taken us and set us in the exact place He wants us to be.

Nothing can move us because we are right where God has placed us. Sickness comes, we are still here. Adversity comes, we remain. Financial crisis comes, we're still in right standing.

Now if the devil can get us out of our God-ordained position, then he can defeat us. But as long as we are in right standing, in right position, we are like a tree planted by the rivers of water. We shall not be moved. There is divine determination in our destiny.

Those God justifies, He glorifies. The word *glorify* means "to make light, to clear or clarify, to make luminous, to make transparent, to make obvious." We take the place of Lucifer. We are light. Lucifer is not. His name is Satan now, but he used to be Lucifer, which means "light bearing."[1]

Now it is very clear and very obvious who we are. And we're in the right place. So every time the devil sees us he says, "There's one of them. I can't mess with him as long as he's in right standing with God. He's already justified. I can tell because he's glowing. He's anointed. His

---

[1]*Smith's Bible Dictionary* (Philadelphia: A. J. Holman Company), p. 156.

countenance speaks the glory of the Lord. No matter how much darkness I put around him, I can still see him. He's one of them."

If God is for us, who can be against us? We may have suffered defeat and loss in the past. We may have miscarried in days gone by. But we are still God's called, chosen, ordained, anointed, and destined people. There is still within us room for a new vision, for the new wind of the Holy Ghost.

This is a new day in Jesus Christ, and nothing is going to stop us this time. I want you to join me in the lap of sovereignty and rest. It's all right to be concerned, but let's not worry. I've got a feelin' everything's gonna be all right!

8
The Crucified Life

Therefore, since we have been justified through faith, we have peace with God through our Lord Jesus Christ.

Romans 5:1

The word *justified* means "made innocent or acquitted."

As believers in Jesus Christ, our sins have been remitted. We have been put in right position, right posture, right relationship with God. Since we have been put in right standing with the Lord, through our faith in His Son, Jesus Christ, we have peace.

That word *peace* in Greek suggests "to set at one." We have become one with God. We have rest from the pain of separation. Rest from the pain of being out of fellowship. We are once again with and in God.

There are lots of people who are experiencing a tremendous strain in their relationship with God. Most Christians go around thinking that God is angry with them, that He is upset with them because they have failed to go to church, fast, pray, read the Scriptures, pay their tithe, or witness to others. They pray and ask forgiveness and end up feeling miserable because they just know that things aren't right between them and the Lord. Subconsciously they feel a sense of guilt, of alienation and separation.

What does it take to change that feeling?

God's Grace

Through whom we have gained access by faith into this grace in which we now stand. And we rejoice in the hope of the glory of God.

Romans 5:2

The Apostle Paul says that we have peace with God through the Lord Jesus Christ through Whom we have gained access to God by faith into this grace. That word *grace* actually means *graciousness*.

God is gracious. He is kind. He is gratuitous. And because of our faith in Jesus Christ, we now stand in God's gratuity. God's favor. It is by grace through faith that we have been accepted by God. (Eph. 2:8.) And now we have peace by grace. All we can do is rejoice, all we can say is, "Thank You, Lord."

Rejoice in Sufferings

Not only so, but we also rejoice in our sufferings, because we know that suffering produces perseverance; perseverance, character; and character, hope.

Romans 5:3,4

The apostle here suggests that we should glory (rejoice) in sufferings and in tribulation. In Greek these words refer to the things we permit by withstanding. In life there are certain things that we close our eyes, grit our teeth, and endure — things we refuse to yield to though we must suffer through them.

I know what it is to suffer, to endure. I fought for years against becoming pastor of a church. It was not my desire to do so. God called me, and I argued with Him for ten years. But finally I accepted the call. Then I had to contend with the devil. He always tries to tell me that I'm not a pastor. Yet I look around and see the work the Lord has given us through my obedience to Him. But the enemy still attacks and assails me continually.

Sometimes I just have to ignore the things people say and do. Often that is difficult to do. To continue to serve the Lord in the way He has called me, I have to literally grin and bear it. I'm happy to be where I am, but I fight to stay here.

Anyone in a marriage relationship usually has to fight to maintain it. Solomon said, **Enjoy life with your wife, whom you love...**(Eccl. 9:9). That is great wisdom. What he was saying is, live life to the fullest with the commitment you have made.

114

Have you made a commitment? Are you serious about keeping it? Are you locked into a relationship? Are you giving your all to it? Are you enjoying it despite the tribulations and hardships that often accompany it?

Nothing can separate us from the love of God. (Rom. 8:38,39.) That's why I am able to rejoice in the midst of tribulation, because I know that he who has suffered in his flesh has ceased from sin.

Whenever I cease from sin, my flesh protests. It suffers. It doesn't like it because I'm not feeding it. That's why, when you fast, at times your body growls. It tells everybody around you that you haven't fed it. You have to decide to listen to your spirit rather than to your body, which is your nature.

That is the same principle that we are to observe in following and serving the Lord. We are to say no to ungodliness, to sin, to the desires of our lower nature, and yes to the Lord and His will and His desire for us. We overcome sin and lust by living on a higher plane — a spiritual level. It is truly a higher dimension!

I fast often. I'm always fasting something, but not always food. I continually deny myself something because if I don't, my body will get out of hand. My flesh will start dictating to me. None of us needs or wants a fleshly dictator oppressing and controlling our lives.

Remember, sin came into this world through our mouths, our appetites, through our desire for fleshly gratification. So when you make up your mind that you're going to resist that temptation, you are exercising spiritual power. That is the purpose and strength of fasting. It dramatizes the sincerity of your prayer and brings the body into subjection to the Holy Spirit. You become a different person. It literally humbles you. It makes you different. If the saints of God would fast and pray more, a whole new spiritual dimension would be opened to us, and we would enjoy a fresh new demeanor and way of life.

But the answer is not just a fast of food, it is a fasted life, which means a continual and ongoing lifestyle of consecration and special devotion to God.

I am a normal human being with all the appetites and desires and tendencies of a man of my age. I have to deal with that. How? The weapons of my warfare are not carnal, but mighty through God. Although I suffer in my body, I do not yield to it and its desires and dictates. Sometimes my body flinches, it argues with me. But like the Apostle Paul, I keep my flesh under subjection lest it gain the dominance over me.

The conflict we endure in a physical fast is just an outward sign of the battle we all fight within. Don't think for one second that when Jesus came out of the wilderness of temptation, in which He hadn't eaten in forty days, that He was not hungry and physically weak. The devil knew He was weak and hungry so he said to Him, "If You are the Son of God, turn those stones into bread." But the Lord said in essence, "My appetite must be brought under subjection to the Holy Ghost. I have bread that you know nothing about." (John 4:32.)

That must be our response to the temptation which we must face as believers. We must not fall for the delusion that because we are under grace, we can go on sinning without consequence. The Church of Jesus Christ will never accomplish the work the Lord has preordained for it until it first learns to overcome the evil within through patient suffering.

In Romans 5:3 Paul tells us that suffering produces perseverance. The King James Version of this passage says, ...tribulation worketh patience. In Greek the word translated perseverance or patience means "cheerful endurance."

Suffering or tribulation produces in us cheerful endurance; and cheerful endurance — which means that our attitude suggests how we endure — produces character.

The King James Version translates it experience. But the word means "a proving of." It really means "proof through trial."

After we have been tested, we have character. And character then produces hope, a happy anticipation of good.

The Spirit Within

And hope does not disappoint us, because God has poured out his love into our hearts by the Holy Spirit, whom he has given us.

Romans 5:5

In my spirit I am enjoying my journey to heaven. Thank God for the Holy Ghost Who is my joy. He gives me joy that is unspeakable, which means that sometimes I can't verbalize it. It's just deep down on the inside. It doesn't make sense, but I'm happy. I'm fighting a battle, but I'm happy. I get kicked around and I sustain injuries from demonic battles, but I'm rejoicing anyway!

I enjoy the peace that passes all understanding. I've got peace, and I can't even understand why I have it. I've got joy, but I can't describe what it's like. It's not the joy that the world has. It's another kind of joy — supernatural joy.

I'm human. Yes, I have a body. Yes, I have a mind. But I am a spirit and the weapons of my warfare are spiritual and powerful. The devil has won some battles, but he is not winning the war.

I'm in for the long haul. I'm not about to give up. We stumble sometimes. We fumble the ball on occasion. But we are justified by faith. That means that because we are justified, we are no longer under condemnation. (Rom. 8:1.) Instead, I am in Christ Jesus, and I walk not after the flesh but after the Spirit. The Holy Spirit indwells and enlightens me. He empowers me to say no to the flesh and yes to the things of God.

There should be no sin in our lives or shame in our hearts because we have been given the power of the Holy

Ghost to overcome temptation, and the presence of the Holy Ghost to assure us of our acceptance by God as His beloved sons and daughters — those He has redeemed from sin and death.

Christist Died for Us

> You see, at just the right time, when we were still powerless, Christ died for the ungodly. Very rarely will anyone die for a righteous man, though for a good man someone might possibly dare to die. But God demonstrates his own love for us in this: While we were still sinners, Christ died for us.
>
> **Romans 5:6-8**

Just at the right time, when we were weak and powerless to help ourselves, Christ died for us. What kind of lives ought we then lead now that we have become the righteousness of God in Him? Shall we continue to sin that grace may abound? God forbid!

Justified and Reconciled

> Since we have now been justified by his blood, how much more shall we be saved from God's wrath through him! For if, when we were God's enemies, we were reconciled to him through the death of his Son, how much more, having been reconciled, shall we be saved through his life! Not only is this so, but we also rejoice in God through our Lord Jesus Christ, through whom we have now received reconciliation.
>
> **Romans 5:9-11**

We are justified (are in right standing with God) by the blood of Christ. We have been reconciled to God. Why then should we feel any shame, guilt, remorse, dread, or fear? Why should we feel alienated or separated from God? He loves us, and we are His.

Live by the Spirit

So I say, live by the Spirit, and you will not gratify the desires of the sinful nature.

Galatians 5:16

The great aim of religion is fellowship with God. The great problem with religion is sin which interrupts that fellowship. That is what Paul is warning us about in his letter to the Galatians. The *King James Version* of this passage says, **. . . Walk in the Spirit, and ye shall not fulfil the *lust* of the flesh.**

It is very easy to say, ''Lord, I've given You my whole life. I pray, I preach, I am a missionary, an evangelist. I testify, I give, I fast. But there's one little area I get personal pleasure from and I know it's wrong, but please give me some slack, Lord. I'm doing everything else right, and You know my heart. I'm never going to backslide completely. But there is this one area that. . . I don't know. . . I think it must be a thorn in my flesh.''

This is how Christians fail, especially preachers with powerful, successful ministries that help lots of people. They try to justify their sins and errors by their good deeds. The enemy whispers to them, ''Look, just hang in there, and don't make an issue of this thing. Paul had a thorn, David fell into sin, Solomon messed up, Samson got into trouble with Delilah, even Abraham lied. None of them was one hundred percent right and pure, so who do you think you are? Be glad that you have your anointing. I won't tell on you. No one ever need know you have this one little private indiscretion.''

He starts talking to you this way when you are young and unknown, while you're still fasting and praying and working for the Lord. Then when you begin to mature and expand he says, ''See how you're growing. The whole world is watching you. You're sending millions to missions, preaching to thousands. They're asking for you all over the world. Has this little thing been a problem to you so far?

You've been doing it all along. Nobody even knows about it."

It's all a ruse of the devil. He is lying in wait until the minister gets big and commanding, when all eyes are on him. Then Satan pulls the carpet out from under him and he falls with a thud — and the whole earth reverberates with his failure.

Some of that has already happened. The enemy is patient. He'll wait twenty-five years. But before it's over, he's going to expose the one who is foolish enough to fall for his deception. If he can't stop a person from preaching and ministering in public, he'll corrupt him in private.

He says, "I'll let you preach and minister under the anointing. I'll let you sing and play the instruments. I'll let you have a great ministry. But just give me a little space. I don't want your whole life; I just want a little bit of your time. Why not? After all, nobody's perfect."

Have you heard that voice before? The Scriptures say to give the devil no place. (Eph. 4:27.) Jesus told the devil, "Get thee behind me, Satan! I want you out of My mind, My will. You cannot dominate My flesh. I am not going to fulfill the lust of My flesh, but I will walk in the Spirit."

God has never said that the lusts of the flesh are not real, or that they will not bother us. He just said that we are not to give in to them. We don't have to fulfill the lusts of the flesh if we live by the Spirit and are led by Him day by day.

Led by the Spirit

For the sinful nature desires what is contrary to the Spirit, and the Spirit what is contrary to the sinful nature. They are in conflict with each other, so that you do not do what you want. But if you are led by the Spirit, you are not under law.

Galatians 5:17,18

There is always a conflict. Always. There is always a battle. But if you are led by and yielded to the Holy Ghost, then you're not under the law (standards) of sin and death. Instead, you are led by the higher law. The law that is within. It's not written in tablets of stone, it's written in tablets of human hearts. (2 Cor. 3:3.)

Works Vs. Fruit

The acts of the sinful nature are obvious: sexual immorality, impurity and debauchery; idolatry and witchcraft; hatred, discord, jealousy, fits of rage, selfish ambition, dissensions, factions and envy; drunkenness, orgies, and the like. I warn you, as I did before, that those who live like this will not inherit the kingdom of God.

But the fruit of the Spirit is love, joy, peace, patience, kindness, goodness, faithfulness, gentleness, and self-control. Against such things there is no law.
Galatians 5:19-23

It doesn't matter how well you sing, or how anointed you appear to be, the gifts of God are without repentance. (Rom. 11:29.) That means that they're irrevocable. Once you're called and gifted, God does not change His mind. You have the gift. Even if you continually sin, you still have the gift. But just because you sing, preach, pray, or exercise gifts of the Spirit doesn't mean that you're going to heaven. (Matt. 7:15-23.)

The Lord didn't say that we will know His servants by their gifts, He said that we will know them by their fruits.

So when you see someone very gifted and anointed, and you find out that he or she is not as holy and straight as you thought, don't be misled or confused concerning God's choices. Don't make excuses for the individual just because of the great work that is being done in his or her ministry. Good works and great achievements are not to be confused with the fruit of the Spirit.

Crucified With Christ

Those who belong to Christ Jesus have crucified the sinful nature with its passions and desires.

Galatians 5:24

Paul said that we are to crucify our sinful nature. Jesus told us to take up our cross daily. (Luke 9:23.) In our lives as Christians, there must be a daily crucifixion, a daily death to the sinful nature with its passions and wrong desires. Crucifixion was a slow and painful form of execution. Daily crucifixion is not supposed to be pleasant. Only the Holy Spirit enables us to carry it out. Trust Him.

In Step With the Spirit

Since we live by the Spirit, let us keep in step with the Spirit.

Galatians 5:25

If we truly want to follow and serve the Lord, let's learn to crucify the flesh. Let's learn to keep in step with the Spirit.

9

What Spirit Are We of?

I have been reading a book, *The Day America Told the Truth* (written by James Patterson and Peter Kim; published by Prentice Hall Press in New York, New York; copyrighted © 1991). It is on the market at the time of this writing and is getting a lot of media coverage.

This book is very sobering to anybody who reads it. In this chapter I am going to highlight some of the major revelations contained in this work because I think they are important to the Church and its role and function in our modern-day society.

The authors of this book interviewed or surveyed about five thousand Americans in different regions of the continent, individuals of different races, cultures and social and intellectual levels. By analyzing the answers they received to some eighteen hundred questions, they were able to provide a pretty fair overview of the way America looks at things.

Let's consider some of their findings as they relate to us in the Body of Christ today. I have listed these revelations by their numerical order in the book. This is not necessarily my opinion. It is what the survey reported.

Women Are More Moral Than Men

The number one revelation of this study is that in America women are morally superior to men. This fact is true all across the country, everywhere, in every single region and on every moral issue tested. Both sexes say so emphatically.

The survey reports that women lie less. Women are more responsible, more honest at work. Women can be trusted more.

The implication is, of course, that women should be looked to for leadership. Right now very few women are in real leadership positions in America. That situation should be changed. That was the overall feeling of the people surveyed.

A Lack of Moral Leadership

The number two revelation, according to the survey, Americans feel that at this time our nation has no strong leaders, and especially no strong moral leadership. Americans across the board believe that the current political, religious, and business leaders have failed us miserably and completely.

I was in New Orleans some time ago when two nationally prominent preachers were bickering publicly and filing countersuits against each other. I resented that situation because it is not of God. It is against Scripture. Such conflicts should be settled out of court, not in the public eye.

The only reason I'm addressing this issue so openly is that no one else has done so to my knowledge. Not many seem to know the difference between right and wrong in this kind of situation.

The newscasters asked one of the preachers involved, "Couldn't this matter be settled out of court?"

"I don't want it settled out of court," the man answered. "I want to go through with the thing. If my insurance company pays one dime, I'll sue them."

That kind of arrogance has no place in the Body of Christ. If that is the way our religious leaders believe and behave, what can we expect from the rank and file of their followers?

People in our society are going in all different directions because they don't know what's right and what's wrong. We've lost our conscience because we have no moral base.

At this time, America has few really strong leaders, especially moral ones. Our void in leadership, morally and otherwise, has reached a critical stage. We still want strong leadership. We just can't find it. That's what the people of our nation are saying.

Americans want real leaders, leaders to address the difficult issues and decide what's right and what isn't. Whether they agree with the decisions reached or not, people want some type of guidance. When senators are corrupt and congressmen are irresponsible, when sheriffs and police officers and judges and doctors and attorneys and corporate executives and preachers fail, where does that leave a generation that is looking for leadership and guidance?

May God raise up today a new standard for leadership, a new anointing for biblical morality.

America needs revival, and she needs it now. Out there somewhere there is still a "moral majority," a broad-based segment of our population that is clean, decent, and honest. But they are not necessarily organized. Maybe they don't need to be organized. We just need the spirit of morality through the Church — not through parachurch organizations, but through the church, the local church. Every preacher in America ought to deal with sin in his own life first and then in the lives of his congregation.

A Lack of Moral Self-Determination

A third observation noted in this survey was: Americans are making up their own rules. They're making up their own laws, in effect, because they don't trust their elected and appointed officials anymore. The recent exposure of police brutality in Los Angeles, and other such incidents, can be overblown by the media and the public, of course. But they have created a certain amount of disrespect for the law in our society at all levels.

Not long ago we learned from the media that a fourteen-year-old boy, completely nude and bleeding from the rectum as a result of a homosexual assault, was found staggering outside the apartment where the attack had taken place. The police officers who arrived on the scene didn't do anything about it because they assumed it was just a "homosexual lovers' quarrel" and chose not to get involved. They, in essence, sent the boy back to his deranged captor, who was later discovered to be a mass murderer, a butcher whose home was littered with the dismembered parts of eleven victims, including the boy himself. That is not only tragic, it is criminal.

The police are what we preachers are. Where the police aren't guarding lives, the preachers aren't guarding souls. We are dealing with sin too lightly. We're casually acting as though it doesn't exist, while people are on their way to hell. Someone has got to speak up. Somebody needs to say something. People are waiting to hear a word from the Lord.

We in the Body of Christ have believed, we have stood on the Word, we have confessed, we have prospered, we have done well — for ourselves. But in the meanwhile, we have allowed Satan and his demons to run amok not only in our society but even in the Church itself. That must stop.

When God began to give me this message to deliver, I said, "Lord, I don't want to preach this. You're blessing my ministry. Why can't I just speak on some nice, safe, non-controversial topic?"

And the devil said, "Yes, that's right. I won't bother you one bit as long as you talk about something else, but don't talk about sin. I'll let your meetings be full to overflowing, I'll allow the anointing to rest upon you unhindered. I won't interfere at all. Just don't deal with me. Let me do my thing, and I'll let you do yours."

Well, part of "my thing" is dealing with sin and calling it by its name.

The holiness of God finds its most articulate expression in condemnation of sin. As has been said, the great aim of religion is fellowship with God; the great problem with religion is sin, which interrupts that fellowship.

God is saying to the Church today: "If my people who are called by My name would humble themselves and pray and seek My face and turn from their wicked ways, then their prayers would no longer be hindered and revival would come." (2 Chron. 7:14.)

Americans are making up their own rules, their own laws, and we are making up our own moral codes. Only thirteen percent of us believe in all the Ten Commandments. Forty percent of us believe in five of the Ten Commandments. We choose which laws of God we believe and which we don't. There's absolutely no moral consensus in this country as there was in the 1950s when all our institutions commanded more respect. Today there is very little respect for the law, for any kind of law — moral, ethical, legislative, or spiritual.

Young Males Cause Crime

The fourth disturbing revelation of this survey is this: Young American males are our biggest national tragedy. In this statement no reference is made to race, color, culture, or social status, only to gender and age — just to young American males in general between the ages of eighteen and twenty-five.

This group is the real cause of our overwhelming crime problem. That's where most of the crimes are perpetrated, within that age group of males.

We don't have good strong male role models in our society today. Many of our athletes, rock musicians, and movie idols are arrogant, boastful, and self-indulgent. They're overpaid and underdisciplined. They're taking drugs. They're fighting. They're being dishonest. They're violent, untrustworthy, and undependable.

At one time our young men were disciplined in the military before joining the ranks of the civilian population. But no more. Now they have become our greatest cause and source of violent crime.

Men Vs. Women

Number five: a men's revolution is bubbling below the surface of American society. It is coming as a strong reaction to the women's revolution. Many men now feel that women are using them for selfish or frivolous reasons. I'm not saying that this is necessarily true. This is what is being said based on observation and inquiry.

I believe this is one cause for an increase in homosexuality. Because we don't understand the roles between male and female, husband and wife, mother and father, people are confused and mixed up.

Recently I saw a male choir on television. It was one of the most beautiful sounding musical groups I have ever heard. It was made up of handsome, strong-looking men who are all practicing homosexuals. They are going throughout the country sharing their great talents, but at the same time they are saying: "Accept us as we are. There's nothing wrong with us, even if we have lesions on our faces, even if we are dying with AIDS. Don't reject us simply because we have chosen a different lifestyle."

A person cannot lead an absolutely abominable lifestyle, one that is against the laws of nature and of God, and expect the favor of the Lord to be upon him.

We in the Church love homosexuals, but we don't love homosexuality. We love sinners, but we don't love sin.

Somebody has got to call sin by its name. What does the Bible say about all this? What does it say about fornication, adultery, homosexuality, lesbianism? It says that it is of the flesh.

We need deliverance as a nation. That deliverance can only come through the Lord Jesus Christ. A local church must be full of Jesus: living, teaching, and preaching His mighty power to save and deliver.

Social Morality Has Replaced Personal Righteousness

Revelation six: The 1990s will be marked by moral crusades.

Millions of dollars are being spent on AIDS research, housing for the homeless, food for the poor, and other social welfare programs. Many thousands of people are offering their support, free of charge, to aid in the betterment of our society. Yet there is still an appalling lack of personal righteousness among our people.

Many Americans ache to do the right thing but feel that there are no outlets through our current institutions. These are not necessarily Christians or atheists, just people of all different backgrounds and viewpoints.

When interviewed, some of these same people told their deepest personal secrets, things they had never even told their spouses, things they had previously not faced themselves. In this book they told about which kind of sex partners they want to have and what kinds of perverted things they want to do — like having sex with children, animals, and multiple partners. Yet they also foresee that the '90s will be marked by moral crusades.

The first moral crusade is actually happening right now. Volunteerism is increasing tremendously. In this decade we're going to hear "save the land, clothe the children, feed the hungry, care for the AIDS patients." Everybody is getting into volunteerism.

That is all well and good, but what we need is a good old-fashioned Holy Ghost revival that will sweep our nation from the highest level and throughout.

God is ready to pour out His Spirit upon all flesh. Let's get ready, Church. It's time to get buoyant. It's time to rise like an island in the sea, full of the grace and power of God.

The Lord said to me recently, "My people have continued in sin. They can no longer walk in grace alone. Now they've got to also walk in power, power to resist sin and submit to God, power to live holy every day and in every way.'' (Rom. 6:1-15.)

A Nation of Liars

The seventh revelation is this: Lying has become an integral part of the American culture. Dishonesty is a trait of the American character.

We lie and don't even think about it. We lie for no reason at all. One popular American writer summed it up when he wrote, ''Like most men, I tell a hundred lies a day.'' That's about average, I would say. And the people to whom we lie most regularly are those closest to us.

When the people surveyed were asked the question, ''Who do you lie to most?'' the answer was to their moms and dads and husbands and wives and children and brothers and sisters and best friends.

Parents are lying to their children. Children are lying to parents. Preachers are lying to congregations. Politicians are lying to the public. On and on it goes. How often and how easily we twist the truth to our own advantage.

Abuse Is Rampant in Our Society

Here's revelation number eight: One in seven Americans was sexually abused as a child. And one in six Americans was physically abused as a child.

I don't oppose simple corporal punishment. I think it is healthy and scriptural. This report, however, is referring to real and unfair abuse, including brutality, battering, and violence leading sometimes even to death.

These numbers far exceed official statistics. The U.S. Department of Health and Human Services estimates that approximately 5.7 children per 1,000 in the population have suffered from physical abuse and 2.5 in 1,000 from sexual abuse. However, these estimates are based on official reports only. Most cases of abuse are not reported.

Childhood Has Vanished

Revelation number nine: the ideal childhood has ended.

A startling percentage of American children actually lose their virginity before the age of thirteen.

Remember, this is not a religious study nor a moral appraisal; it is a scientific study, based on actual interviews with Americans of all ages, backgrounds, and walks of life. It shows that our young people are losing their childhood, and losing their innocence, in other ways, too.

Today children are doing and saying things that even my generation was unaware of at that age. And I am not yet forty years old.

Sexual Practices Are Out of Control

The tenth revelation in the survey dealt with sexual violence and perversions. Date rape is the second most important (and largely unreported) epidemic. Twenty percent of the women surveyed reported that they have been raped by their dates.

This revelation contained some further statistics that really staggered me. It records that homosexual fantasies are common in every section of the United States. One in five of us, both men and women, have homosexual fantasies. The authors of the book include a whole chapter just on that one subject.

Forty-two percent of Americans confess to having regular violent sexual urges.

There is in our society an underlying demonic frenzy that has been held at bay thus far only by the Church. If we continue to loosen the moral restraints, this nation will explode into the most heinous crimes in its history.

There Is a Breakdown of Marriage and Family

Revelation eleven: While Americans still marry, they have lost faith in the institution of marriage.

A third of married men and women confess that they have had at least one extramarital affair. Thirty percent aren't sure that they really love their spouse. Fifty-two percent of all new marriages end in divorce. And among black women, fifty percent of the babies born are born out of wedlock.

I don't put the blame for the situation on race. It's not a problem of skin; it's a problem of sin.

There is also a breakdown in what I call "philiopiety." A majority of us will not take care of our parents in their old age. There is so much bitterness in people toward their parents. There's so much hurt between family members.

Recently I was watching a popular talk show dealing with this topic. The host asked a lady if her husband were dying and she had a little savings, would she spend it on helping him get cured. She said, "No, I would let the man die, because he's going to anyway."

Another person was asked, "Would you spend your inheritance or life savings to take care of your parents?" The answer was no.

Right or wrong, that would not have been said thirty years ago.

An Unethical Society

Twelve: The number one cause of our business decline is low ethics by executives. Who says so? Executives themselves and workers.

Sixty-eight percent of us don't believe that America has a single hero right now. A let-down in moral values is now considered the primary problem facing our country. Eighty percent of us believe that morals and ethics should be taught in our schools again. I hope every senator and congressman in the nation reads that statistic.

Please pay careful attention to what I'm saying. Many people are intolerant of truth. They don't want to deal with the issues that face us. But we in the Church must face these issues and deal with them spiritually and scripturally.

Sin and Death

Therefore, just as sin entered the world through one man, and death through sin, and in this way death came to all men, because all sinned.

Romans 5:12

When Adam chose to disobey God, sin — the entity of sin, the spirit of sin, the plague and curse of sin — entered the world. Sin spread to all people, and as a result, death came upon everyone, because all of us have sinned.

Because of the inherited Adamic nature, everybody came into this world in the status of sin, even before he ever committed a sin. Then when each person committed the act of sin, the state of his spirit became that of a sinner.

The Gift of Grace

For before the law was given, sin was in the world. But sin is not taken into account where there is no law. Nevertheless, death reigned from the time of Adam to the time of Moses [when the law was given], **even over those who did not sin by breaking a command, as did Adam, who was a pattern of the one to come** [Jesus Christ].

But the gift [the charisma, the gift of grace] **is not like the trespass** [or the offense]. **For if the many died by the trespass** [or failure or offense] **of the one man** [Adam], **how much more did God's grace and the gift that came by the grace of the one man, Jesus Christ, overflow to the many!**

Romans 5:13-15

In other words, if all of the human race is subjected to death because of one man's status, then why can't all of us be subjected to grace because of Jesus Christ?

God is a just God. That means that He cannot wink at or disregard sin. But He is also a merciful God, which

133

means that He has to find a way to save mankind, because He is so full of love for His creation.

Between justice and mercy is grace. Grace understands God's justice and His mercy. And we call it amazing.

The gift, the grace, the *charis* of God, is not like the trespass. The judgment followed one sin and brought condemnation, which means that sentence was passed, a verdict was pronounced upon man. But the gift followed many trespasses and brought justification to man.

For if by the trespass of one man death dominated or reigned or ruled through that one man, how much more will those who have received God's abundant provision of grace and of the gift of right standing, or right status, reign in life through one man, Jesus Christ.

The difference between the status of sin and the state of sin is our deeds.

Grace Says No to Sin

For the grace of God that brings salvation has appeared to all men. It teaches us to say "No" to ungodliness and worldly passions, and to live self-controlled, upright and godly lives in this present age, while we wait for the blessed hope — the glorious appearing of our great God and Savior, Jesus Christ, who gave himself for us to redeem us from all wickedness and to purify for himself a people that are his very own, eager to do what is good.

Titus 2:11-14

The grace of God, the *charis*, the gratuitous kindness of God, has appeared and gives us the wherewithal to say no. Not just to say, "Because of grace I'm going to continue in sin." It enables us to "just say no!"

The Spirit of the Lord actually gives us the power to say, "I am a changed entity. There is no hostility between God and me. I will not engage in sin because I want to live a self-controlled, upright, and godly life in this present age, while I wait for my blessed hope — the glorious appearing of my great God and Savior, Jesus Christ, Who has redeemed me from all wickedness and sin.''

From Sinners to the Righteous

For if, by the trespass of the one man, death reigned through that one man, how much more will those who receive God's abundant provision of grace and of the gift of righteousness reign in life through the one man, Jesus Christ.

Consequently, just as the result of one trespass was condemnation for all men, so also the result of one act of righteousness was justification that brings life for all men. For just as through the disobedience of the one man the many were made sinners, so also through the obedience of the one man the many will be made righteous.

Romans 5:17-19

Just as through the disobedience of the one man, Adam, many were made or designated or ordained sinners, so through the obedience of one man, Jesus Christ, many were made or can be designated righteous.

We who are in Christ are no longer classified as sinners, now we are classified as righteous. How then should we, the righteous ones, live?

Shall We Go on Sinning?

...Shall we go on sinning so that grace may increase? By no means! We died to sin; how can we live in it any longer?

Romans 6:1,2

If we are already declared righteous, should we be content to go on sinning so that God's grace may abound? Paul gives an emphatic ''No!'' He says that we are dead to sin; how then can we go on living in it?

Sin Is Not Our Master

In the same way, count yourselves dead to sin but alive to God in Christ Jesus. Therefore do not let sin

> reign in your mortal body so that you obey its evil desires. Do not offer the parts of your body to sin, as instruments of wickedness, but rather offer yourselves to God, as those who have been brought from death to life; and offer the parts of your body to him as instruments of righteousness. For sin shall not be your master, because you are not under law, but under grace.
>
> **Romans 6:11-14**

Since I have been redeemed by the blood of Christ, I count myself dead to sin — out of accordance or out of correspondence with sin — but alive to God in Christ Jesus. Therefore, I will not let sin reign, govern, rule, dictate, monopolize, or manipulate my mortal body so that I obey its evil desires.

Sin has evil desires and I have a fleshly nature, but I am not going to yield to it. The Holy Ghost is helping me resist that spirit that wants me to compromise.

Note that in Verse 14 Paul tells us that since we have been declared righteous, since we are under grace and not the law, that does not mean that we have a license to sin, but that we have an obligation to live holy to God, and to disallow sin to be our master.

We Are Not Controlled by Sin

> You, however, are controlled not by the sinful nature but by the Spirit, if the Spirit of God lives in you. And if anyone does not have the Spirit of Christ, he does not belong to Christ.
>
> **Romans 8:9**

I have a sinful nature, but by the grace of God and the power of the Holy Ghost, I am not controlled by that nature. Rather I am controlled by the Spirit of God Who lives in me.

If anyone does not have the Spirit of Christ — that is, the breath or life of Christ — he does not belong to Christ.

Alive to the Spirit

But if Christ is in you, your body is dead because of sin, yet your spirit is alive because of righteousness. And if the Spirit of him who raised Jesus from the dead is living in you, he who raised Christ from the dead will also give life to your mortal bodies through his Spirit, who lives in you.

Romans 8:10,11

In other words, if we are in Christ and His Spirit is in us, we are mortal without being sinful.

You and I are exempt from mortal liabilities. Greater is He Who is in us than he who is in the world. (1 John 4:4.) Our body is the temple of the Holy Ghost. (1 Cor. 3:16.) We are not our own. We have been bought with a price, paid for by the blood of the Lamb. (1 Cor. 6:19,20.)

"It is not by might nor by power," says the Lord, "but by My Spirit that you are to live." (Zech. 4:6.)

We Are Sons of God

Therefore, brothers, we have an obligation — but it is not to the sinful nature, to live according to it. For if you live according to the sinful nature, you will die; but if by the Spirit you put to death the misdeeds of the body, you will live, because those who are led by the Spirit of God are sons of God.

Romans 8:12-14

I am a debtor. I am in debt. But not to my flesh. I don't owe the flesh anything. Jesus paid it all, all to *Him* I owe.

You have a debt, but it's not to the sinful nature. If you live in accordance to it, if you correspond with your sinful nature, you will die. But if, by the Holy Ghost, you put to death — you stop corresponding with — the misdeeds of the flesh or the body, you will live.

Because those who are led by the Spirit of God are offspring — name and nature bearers — of God. Those of us who are led and driven and compelled and controlled

137

and manipulated by the Holy Ghost, we are the sons of God. Not just children, sons.

I am my father's son. I'm also my mother's son. But I inherited my father's name: Pearson. My mother's maiden name is Johnson, like her father's name was Johnson. Though I received my mother's genes and chromosomes, and I love the ground she walks on, I take my identity from my father.

We are the sons and daughters of our heavenly Father, which means that we fall heir, not only to His name, but also to the promise, to the power, to the hope, to His nature. That means that we are somebody. We are to carry on the family name, the legacy, of our Father in heaven. Can we do that and still engage in sin, still be subject to the god of this world? Are we sons and daughters of Satan? Did we inherit his name, his nature, his spirit?

The Spirit of Sonship

For you did not receive a spirit that makes you a slave again to fear, but you received the Spirit of sonship. And by him we cry, *"Abba,* Father." The Spirit himself testifies with our spirit that we are God's children. Now if we are children, then we are heirs — heirs of God and co-heirs with Christ, if indeed we share in his sufferings in order that we may also share in his glory.

Romans 8:15-17

Sonship. That word doesn't mean that we are suddenly made perfect overnight so that we don't make any more mistakes. We will still err and fall into temptation. The difference is that we will not continue to live in sin because now we have a new identity, a new nature, a new Spirit Who lives within us and Who leads us not into temptation, but delivers us from evil, and Who guides us into all truth.

America is tired and ready for revival. So is the Church. So am I. Can I make you a promise? It's coming. It's coming through you and me. As I explained earlier, the grace of God, in which many have lived and carelessly sinned, is going to be lifted so that in the coming months we are going to witness the exposure of many things that are going to embarrass and convict us. If Christians don't walk in power as well as grace, they will walk into forbidden territory — and be exposed and destroyed. Again, ...**Shall we go on sinning so that grace may increase? By no means!**... (Rom. 6:1,2).

We must not continue sinning. We need somebody to give us an intelligent exhortation on what true holiness really is, for no one who wilfully lives in sin will recognize God — or His great move — in these last days. Instead he will be blinded and deadened to truth and light. But the righteous will shine like the sun in the Kingdom of their Father. (Matt. 13:43.)

10
Struggling With Sin

The word *sin* means "to miss the mark" or "to fall short of the goal." It isn't just fornication, adultery, robbing, lying, stealing. Those are symptoms of sin.

To *sin* really means "to fall short of what God intends for us to be." Morally, physically, intellectually, and spiritually — every part of our triune being. So although we have been made the righteousness of God in Christ, we still have to deal with the issue of sin.

If we can get the right focus on our commitment to Christ, it is much easier to live a life of victory in compliance with the wishes and leadings of the Holy Spirit Who indwells us. As we stated earlier, the Holy Ghost governs, He doesn't rule us in the sense that sin does. Sin is dictatorial. Sin is tyrannical. It pays wages, and the wages are death. But the gift of God is eternal life. The Holy Spirit governs our life only to the degree that we cooperate with Him once we have submitted to the Lordship of Jesus Christ.

So now, since we have made our commitment to the Lord to live in accordance with His will and plan for our lives, sin has taken on a new aspect or dimension. As Christians, dedicated and committed to the Lord, the question we have been forced to consider is the one posed to the Roman believers by the Apostle Paul.

Shall We Sin?

What then? Shall we sin because we are not under law but under grace? By no means!

Romans 6:15

Many of us were raised in legalism. Today many people have rebelled against that over-emphasis upon strict standards of holiness and don't want to hear anything about it at all. Their claim is: "We're under grace, not the law. We have lost our sin consciousness. We are the righteousness of God in Christ Jesus. Therefore, we have

141

no sin problem. It was all taken care of on the cross of Calvary. So why should we even think about sin?''

Because of that kind of teaching and attitude, sin has run rampant through the Church, from our most notable leaders all the way down and through the Body of Christ. The result has been that many people have gotten discouraged and given up. They have concluded that all Christians, especially ministers, are hypocrites, that they have backslidden and fallen away. They have become cynical and critical of the Church and Christianity. So somebody needs to address this issue of sin openly and forcefully.

Whether we like hellfire and brimstone preaching or not is not the point. We have a responsibility as ministers of the Gospel to deal with sin and its nature and consequences. Just as Paul had to do in his day, I must continue to call attention to a question which has to be addressed and corrected.

Whose Slaves Are We?

Don't you know that when you offer yourselves to someone to obey him as slaves, you are slaves to the one whom you obey — whether you are slaves to sin, which leads to death, or to obedience, which leads to righteousness?

Romans 6:16

Paul tells us that we are going to be slaves either to sin, which leads to death, or to obedience which leads to righteousness.

That word *obedience* means ''giving ear to, accepting as valid or truthful, yielding mentally.'' *Righteousness* is defined as ''the character of being right or just, correctly positioned with God.''

Who do we think we are fooling? Who will believe our claims to be the righteousness of God in Christ if our attitudes and actions provide unmistakable evidence that we are still slaves to sin and Satan?

Set Free From Sin

But thanks be to God that, though you used to be slaves to sin, you wholeheartedly obeyed the form of teaching to which you were entrusted [that is, the Gospel]. **You have been set free from sin and have become slaves to righteousness.**

Romans 6:17,18

You and I have been exempted from the mortal liabilities of sin. We have become slaves of righteousness. We are in bondage to righteousness.

Paul is declaring to us that we are no longer under obligation to sin. Since we are saved, dead to sin in our mortal bodies but alive to Christ in our spirits, sin is no longer relevant to us. It doesn't relate to us. It has no restraint on us anymore since we have been set free from the law of sin and death.

We have now been restrained to righteousness. That doesn't mean that we'll never make an error, but when we do, we will know that we have done so. We will not be happy with our mistake or failure. We will be sorry. We will be repentant in our heart, and change.

In simplest terms, to *repent* really means "to stop and change direction, to go another way." Now when we fall into sin and error, we will change course — in order to avoid that same snare or obstacle in the future. We will still sin, but we will not continue to *live* in sin.

Weak in Flesh, Strong in Spirit

I put this in human terms because you are weak in your natural selves. Just as you used to offer the parts of your body in slavery to impurity and to ever-increasing wickedness, so now offer them in slavery to righteousness leading to holiness.

Romans 6:19

Paul says that he has to speak to us in human terms because we are weak in our natural selves. The *King James Version* says it is because of **the infirmity of your flesh.**

143

I live with the infirmity of my flesh. I know that I am weak in my natural self. But I am strong in my spiritual self.

Paul goes on to tell us that we used to offer the parts of our body to slavery, or subservience to iniquity or impurity, and to ever-increasing wickedness. First, we give our body as slaves to iniquity, then it gets worse.

The horrendous stories coming from the media about mass murderers and their mutilated victims serve to give us a peek at the inside of people who have no moral restraint. They start out with a minor form of passionate crime and end up butchering many people. This kind of spirit is running wild in our society. Every day's news brings to light more and more such gruesome tales. And yet very few people want to address the issue, to get at the real cause of such sickening, disturbing behavior.

Why do people get involved in voyeurism and pornography? Why do people slip around and dabble in secret adulterous romances and illicit affairs? Why do so many people have sinful tendencies to which they yield?

All of us, ministers included, have strong sinful tendencies. All of us must wrestle to keep our body and spirit and mind in line with the will of God. Any of us who lets down his guard will become prey to the strong demonic spirits which are out to tempt, entice, and destroy us. So we need to be warned periodically, perhaps even regularly, to fight the good fight of faith, to lay hold on eternal life, to look at ourselves in the mirror, to see ourselves as we really are, to recognize and acknowledge our sinfulness.

Despite the fact that spiritually we are the righteousness of God in Christ, we must never forget that physically, our normal, carnal nature is weak and hostile toward God and will always resist the Holy Spirit. So we must yield with our will, because our will is stronger than our flesh.

When our will is submitted to the Lord Jesus Christ, we will always have arguments with our flesh. It will growl at us, snarl at us, tug and pull at us. It will not want to yield to God as it should. No matter how strong and righteous and holy we become, temptation will always be there — because in the flesh we are weak.

In my ministry I am often treated like royalty, so I must always be vigilant not to fall into pride, conceit, and arrogance. I am always mindful of the part of Carlton Pearson that would easily yield to sin. I must forever keep my mind and body in check. I don't go around saying, "Praise God, the Lord is with me so much that I am never tempted, never moved by outward influences."

That's a lie. In fact, the more you grow and expand in the ministry, the more susceptible you become to the heavy artillery of the devil. He turns his largest guided missiles on you. It's easy to be humble and prayerful and obedient when nobody knows who you are and what you're doing, when you're seeking to find your place in God and to receive your anointing and commission, when you're struggling to get your ministry launched. But once it gets off the ground and you're soaring like an eagle, then you really need to seek God's face.

That same principle applies to every relationship, such as marriage, even to the relationship you and I have with the Lord Jesus Christ.

The Benefit of Obedience

When you were slaves to sin, you were free from the control of righteousness. What benefit did you reap at that time from the things you are now ashamed of? Those things result in death! But now that you have been set free from sin and have become slaves to God, the benefit you reap leads to holiness, and the result is eternal life. For the wages of sin is death, but the gift of God is eternal life in Christ Jesus our Lord.
Romans 6:20-23

Paul tells us to offer the parts of our bodies in slavery to righteousness, which leads to holiness. First there is obedience, which leads to righteousness. Righteousness then leads to holiness. And holiness leads to eternal life.

The Greek word translated *holiness* is **hagiasmos** meaning "to be purified, uncontaminated, separated unto God." In spiritual terms, it really means "to be possessed by God." Separated to Him in conduct befitting those so separated.

You and I are to be *obedient*, which means "to give mental and emotional ascent to an ideal." That obedience leads to *righteousness*, which is "right standing or right positioning with God." Righteousness leads to *holiness*, "total separation to God." And finally, holiness leads to eternal life.

The wages of sin is death (Rom. 6:23), voidness, emptiness, separation, coldness. But the gift of God, the charisma of God, is eternal life through Jesus Christ our Lord.

When something governs you, that means you have a covenant relationship with it. When you are a slave to God, you are in covenant with Him. Don't look at this relationship as bondage, as slavery was portrayed years ago in this country. Don't look upon your slavery to God as if the Holy Ghost is whipping you or forcing you. To be a slave to God simply means that you have entered into a covenant restraint with God.

To *covenant* means literally "to fetter, bind or tie into agreement or commitment."

When you are a slave to righteousness, that means you are in restriction to right positioning with God. That doesn't mean you are perfect, but it means you are constrained to the posture of perfection. To the standard, to the ideology, and to the reality of the truth of God. If you err, it's not your nature, so you repent and get back into proper position. You don't continue in sin, you wrestle to stay in right relationship, in obedience to God, which leads to right standing. That right standing keeps you under God's holiness, and that holiness results in eternal life. But it is a struggle.

Neither Legalistic Nor Sinful

> Do you not know, brothers — for I am speaking to men who know the law — that the law has authority over a man only as long as he lives? For example, by law a married woman is bound to her husband as long as he is alive, but if her husband dies, she is released from the law of marriage. So then, if she marries another man while her husband is still alive, she is called an adulteress. But if her husband dies, she is released from that law and is not an adulteress, even though she marries another man.
>
> Romans 7:1-3

Paul is not making a doctrinal statement here. This is a Jewish man talking to a group of Romans, people who don't understand Hebrew custom and tradition. He points out to them that they are not under the Jewish law now, they are under grace. But at the same time just because they are under grace, he doesn't want them to forget the law or at least the "spirit" of the law (standard).

In essence, he is saying to them, "I don't want you to become legalistic, but I don't want you to become carelessly sinful either. There is a happy medium in there where God can show you how to be moral and yet not be restrained to legalism or religiosity. You can walk in the Spirit and still not fulfill the lust of the flesh."

Quite a little task Paul had — and you and I have. But with the Spirit of God, it can be done.

Legalism Vs. Spiritualism

> So, my brothers, you also died to the law through the body of Christ, that you might belong to another, to him who was raised from the dead, in order that we might bear fruit to God.
>
> Romans 7:4

We died to the law — which is legalism. So now we belong to another, the Lord Jesus Christ — which is spiritualism.

Serving God in the Spirit

For when we were controlled by the sinful nature [the *King James Version* says the flesh], **the sinful passions aroused by the law** [by legalism] **were at work in our bodies, so that we bore fruit for death** [separation, emptiness]. **But now, by dying to what once bound us, we have been released** [delivered, exempted] **from the law so that we serve the new way of the Spirit, and not in the old way of the written** [legalistic] **code.**

Romans 7:5,6

Paul has to be careful in his wording here; otherwise, he is going to make these people too comfortable, and they're going to sin. So although he proclaims to them their freedom from the old legalistic code, he hastens to point out that they are not freed from their obligation to serve the Lord in the new way of the Spirit.

The old way of the written code is gone. I'm not into legalism or religiosity, because I can't handle it. But I must walk in the Spirit where I am empowered to resist temptation and sin. Now that I am free from legalism and religiosity, I follow not an outwardly imposed moral code, but the inward leading of the Spirit of the Living God.

I'm not trying to act out something I am not. I have actually been changed. I yield to the part of me that has been transformed, which is my mind. (Rom. 12:2.)

Your flesh is always somehow enslaved. But your spirit is free. You must let your spirit dominate your flesh. Don't be surprised or discouraged when you are tempted. In fact, temptation ought to give you courage. When you face temptation, something ought to rise up inside you to resist it.

Don't mistake temptation for sin. Don't fall for the old Satanic delusion that if you're tempted you might as well go ahead and sin. Do as the old hymn says and yield not to temptation. Ask the Savior to help you. He will carry you through.

Is the Law Sin?

**What shall we say, then? Is the law sin? Certainly
not! Indeed I would not have known what sin was
except through the law. For I would not have known
what it was to covet if the law had not said, "Do not
covet."**

Romans 7:7

What is the law? It's a principle which governs one's
actions. A standard for the administration of justice or
rightness. What then is the standard for proper Christian
behavior? It is the moral code that God puts in our spirit.
It is not just the written Word, but that which is written
in our own heart, our conscience.

What shall we say then? Is the standard itself sin?
Certainly not! For without that standard we would not have
known what sin was. If there were no rules or standards
or principles, we wouldn't know when we were doing
wrong. Not in the realistic sense. We might feel something
inside, but we would have no real concrete basis for judging
what we feel. If you don't give your child any rules of proper
behavior, how can you say that he is obedient or
disobedient? If there are no standards in the relationship
or home, no system of governing, how can you decide right
or wrong?

That's why God allowed there to be the tree of the
knowledge of good and evil. The forbidden tree in the
middle of the Garden of Eden. Because we are moral
creatures, and it is impossible to be moral without a choice.
So the Lord placed one tree in the garden and commanded
Adam and Eve not to eat from it. He did not do that to tempt
man, but so He could consider him moral and right.

That's the only rule or restriction God placed on
mankind in the garden. Everything else was permissible to
him, that was the original instruction. But the one tree in
the middle of the garden was declared "off limits." Man
was warned by the Lord that if he chose, of his own free

will, to partake of the fruit of that tree, he would die — suffer separation from God.

Man was made initially innocent but not necessarily virtuous. Innocence is the condition of a person before he knows the difference between right and wrong. Virtue is coming face to face with temptation and resisting the evil for the good. Only when we have done that can we be said to be virtuous.

You may be thinking, "I'm neither innocent nor virtuous." In Jesus Christ you're innocent, and through the Holy Spirit you are virtuous. The blood of Jesus Christ restores your innocence, the power of the Holy Ghost gives you virtue — the ability to resist evil. Salvation alone washes you, but the infilling of the Holy Ghost gives you the power to recognize evil and resist it.

Paul says that he would not have known what it was to covet if the law had not said, "Do not covet." The only reason God sent the Ten Commandments is that He was dealing with a group of over two million Jews who had no sense of right and wrong. They had been in Egyptian bondage for four hundred years. They were not organized. They had no system, no rule, no government. So fifty days after they had departed from Egypt, God issued the Ten Commandments to give them some kind of structure or standard.

The only reason the Bible gives us rules and guidelines is to structure the Church so it will not be full of chaos. The reason a man marries one woman and lives with that woman and has children with her, and she with him, is that if we did not have some moral code, we would be like animals, sleeping around with anything and everybody, producing offspring that we don't know. That spirit is already in the world today.

We have allowed a heathenistic, hedonistic spirit to be unleashed upon American society because the Church will not restrain it. We just let it happen. But if men and women of God all over America begin to rise up and preach righteousness under the anointing, we can bind those demonic spirits and turn the whole society around.

Twenty years ago we didn't hear the kind of daily news reports that are broadcast today. We didn't hear of gang wars and murders every day. Violence has become commonplace in our nation — at every level. Rape, incest, abuse of family members and children are of epidemic proportions. Such things are not normal. There's another spirit at work within our society — and we believers are not immune to it. We must be on our guard, forever watchful lest we, too, fall into the kind of bitter, unrestrained, destructive attitude and behavior of the world around us. That's why we have got to yield ourselves to the Holy Spirit.

Don't get careless because you're saved. Those demons are targeting you. When you have committed a repulsive sin, how often do you say to yourself, "What made me say that, do that? I feel cheap, dirty, irresponsible. I can't believe I did that. That wasn't me, Lord. Don't let that thing get hold of me."

Jesus said that we are to pray, ...**lead us not into temptation, but deliver us from evil....** (Matt. 6:13 KJV). What He meant was: "Don't let me get into areas outside my control, but rescue me from the evil one."

Jesus Himself prayed that prayer. Don't think He was never tempted. Scripture tells us that **we have not an high priest which cannot be touched with the feeling of our infirmities; but was in all points tempted like as we are, yet without sin** (Heb. 4:15 KJV). Jesus was tempted, but He didn't sin.

I love that because now I know that He relates to me and my situation, my infirmities, my weakness of the flesh. That's why He sent me the same Holy Spirit He has — to help me resist sin just as He did.

No Law, No Sin

But sin, seizing the opportunity afforded by the commandment, produced in me every kind of covetous

desire. For apart from law, sin is dead.
Romans 7:8

Paul says that without the law he would not have known that covetousness was wrong. But as soon as he learned that from the law, sin began to stir up covetousness within him. For apart from law, sin is dead, it is nonexistent.

The Law Is Holy

Once I was alive apart from law; but when the commandment came, sin sprang to life and I died [I fell out of correspondence with God]. **I found that the very commandment that was intended to bring life actually brought death** [because I could not control myself and resist the sin]. **For sin, seizing the opportunity afforded by the commandment, deceived me, and through the commandment put me to death. So then, the law is holy, and the commandment is holy, righteous and good.**
Romans 7:9-12

So don't put down the law, the commandments, by saying, "I'm not into that; I'm only into grace." Paul said that the law is holy, righteous, and good. In other words, it had and has its God-ordained place and position of significance.

Sin Produces Death

Did that which is good, then, become death to me? By no means! But in order that sin might be recognized as sin, it produced death in me through what was good, so that through the commandment sin might become utterly sinful.
Romans 7:13

Paul is saying that if after you've sinned you don't feel any remorse, then you don't really know you've sinned. So as a Christian, if you sin, then you will feel something. A coldness, a chill, an emptiness, a hollowness, a conviction, a death. That is the Holy Ghost within you. He is not condemning you, but convicting you so you can realize that you have sinned and done wrong.

Sin may feel good in your physical body for a while. But it should never feel good in your spirit. When sin starts feeling good to your spirit, when you no longer feel any sense of remorse for your sins, then you are in real trouble. That's what Paul calls a "reprobate."

Slaves to Sin

We know that the law is spiritual; but I am unspiritual, sold as a slave to sin.

Romans 7:14

The law (the standard or principle) is spiritual. But in our natural state, in our flesh, you and I are not spiritual, we are human, we're carnal. As Paul said, we are (in our flesh) slaves to sin.

The Eternal, Internal Conflict

I do not understand what I do. For what I want to do I do not do, but what I hate I do. And if I do what I do not want to do, I agree that the law is good. As it is, it is no longer I myself who do it, but it is sin living in me. I know that nothing good lives in me, that is, in my sinful nature. For I have the desire to do what is good, but I cannot carry it out.

Romans 7:15-18

As a human being, I have a sinful nature. Sin lives in that nature, and demons try to control that nature. But as a Christian, I have a holy nature, and God the Holy Ghost lives in that nature. The devil is powerful, but God is all-powerful.

There is a war going on within me. The Lord has promised that He will never leave me nor forsake me. He is always with me to help me fight my battles against that other spirit in my other nature. For, like the Apostle Paul, I have the desire to do what is good but I can't carry it out.

It Is Sin Living in Me

For what I do is not the good I want to do; no, the evil I do not want to do — this I keep on doing. Now if I do what I do not want to do, it is no longer I who do it, but it is sin living in me that does it.

Romans 7:19,20

Can you relate to this situation Paul is describing, this inability to do the good that you want to do?

Take your eating habits, for example. Do you have the will power to limit yourself to the right amounts of wholesome, nourishing food? Or are you tempted to overeat or snack all day long? Do you have a habit of cramming into your mouth all kinds of horrible things that you know full well are not good for you? If you know that your overeating and snacking are harmful to you, then why do you do them?

Paul says that it is because of sin that we do such unhealthy things to ourselves, because sin is lurking in our fleshly nature.

The Enemy in the Flesh

So I find this law at work: When I want to do good, evil is right there with me. For in my *inner being* I delight in God's law [God's standards and principles]; but I see another law [another standard or principle] at work in the *members of my body* [in my flesh], waging war against the law of my mind and making me a prisoner of the law of sin at work within my members. What a wretched man I am! Who will rescue me from this body of death? Thanks be to God — through Jesus Christ our Lord!

So then, I myself in my mind am a slave to God's law, but in the sinful nature a slave to the law of sin.

Romans 7:21-25

That word *wretched* means "piercingly, painfully tried."

"O piercingly, painfully tried man that I am! I'm tested and tried. I'm enduring. Who shall rescue me from this deathly nature that I wrestle with day and night?"

And then Paul answers his own question by saying, "Thanks be to God through Jesus Christ the Lord, I am rescued, I am delivered, I am protected, I am preserved from my sinful, deathly nature."

This is a Spirit-filled man. He has been filled with the Holy Ghost for twenty-five years. And yet he states that he has a sinful nature.

No matter how full of the Holy Ghost you are, you will still have a sinful nature that you will have to wrestle against all the days of your life.

If you ever get so self-righteous that you think all you have to do to resist evil is stand and confess and believe, look out! It's not that simple.

We believers are engaged in a great spiritual warfare. If we are to win over sin and Satan, we must put on the whole armor of God and stand firm against the onslaughts of the enemy. The greatest battle we will ever fight will not be against an outward adversary, but against the enemy within — the sin that inhabits our own human nature.

To fulfill our divine calling, we must choose between grace and gravity. We must not use our freedom from the law as an excuse to sin. We must lead the crucified life. We must know what spirit we are of. We must overcome sin and evil with good. We must walk not only in divine health and abundance but also in divine holiness in order to win the world to our Lord and Savior Jesus Christ.

But be of good courage. With God on our side, everything's gonna be all right!

11
Grace or Gravity?

Because we live in a world that appeals to our base nature, and we are citizens of a heavenly kingdom that appeals to our higher nature, we Christians sometimes find ourselves caught in conflict. We are the instruments of righteousness, yet we are the victims of decay. So in the following pages I would like to have a heart-to-heart talk with you from a scriptural perspective concerning what I refer to as grace or gravity.

The Bible says that from the dust we came and to the dust we will return. (Gen. 3:19.) The saddest part of a memorial service is at the grave site, when the preacher very solemnly says, "Ashes to ashes, dust to dust." I hate that part. It seems so final. Yet there is a measure of truth in it, even though we are going to be resurrected. In his letter to the Romans, Paul writes to the believers at Rome on this subject of our flesh and spirit.

The Roman Empire followed the Greek Empire, which started approximately twelve hundred years before Christ. It was during the Roman Empire that Christ was crucified. But a heavy Greek influence of mythology, philosophy, and the fine arts had greatly influenced Rome, just as it has continued to influence all of Western civilization. Historically, this Greek influence has affected our own nation, society, and existence today in a way no other culture has.

Out of the Grecian culture, which was polytheistic (the worship of many gods), grew the Roman culture. So in his letter to the Roman believers, Paul is talking to a group of Christians who do not have a Judaic background. Remember, this is not the Church in Jerusalem, it is the Church in Rome. Christianity is still less than thirty years old. There is no New Testament. All the Bible that exists at this time is the Old Testament, and the people in Rome don't read the Jewish Old Testament. They have no knowledge of it or its teachings.

So here Paul is wrestling with the problem of conveying Judeo-Christian thought to a Gentile, non-Jewish, and virtually non-Christian world, which has no background and understanding of Hebrew history, philosophy, and culture — and thus, no real moral conscience.

Paul's message will relate to us as he deals with the grace of God. The word grace in the Greek New Testament is *charis* which means "gratuitous favor or kindness." *Gravity* in this context can be defined as "that downward, tugging force which all of us combat constantly in our minds and in our bodies." It is the part of us that lusts after sin. It inhabits the flesh. Obviously, being human himself, Paul was personally aware of the warfare that waged between the flesh and the spirit, as we see in his writings.

The Flesh Vs. the Spirit

So I find this law at work: When I want to do good, evil is right there with me. For in my inner being I delight in God's law; but I see another law at work in the members of my body, waging war against the law of my mind and making me a prisoner of the law of sin at work within my members.

Romans 7:21-23

One companion you'll have in life for sure is evil. It will accompany you everywhere, even to a prayer meeting, to a Bible study, to church.

Speaking of this constant companion, Paul says, "When I want to do right, evil is right there with me. However, in my inner being, in my spirit, which has been transformed, I delight in the law or standard or principle of God with my mind. But I find another standard or law or principle at work within my members, my body, my mechanisms. It wars against my mind, making me a prisoner to the standard of sin at work within my members (my human nature)."

This was a man who was filled with the Holy Ghost and who taught the doctrine of it. He had been saved and baptized in the Holy Spirit now for some twenty-five years when he wrote these words.

He was saying, in essence, "Even though I'm filled with the Holy Ghost, and He (the Holy Spirit) governs my life, there's another diabolical ruler who is combating me and trying to make me a prisoner and slave to its dictates."

It doesn't matter how saved, sanctified, and filled with the Holy Ghost you get, you never stop being a human being. That should help explain why some noted evangelists who had a powerful anointing, wonderful preaching ministry, and great command of the Word and of themselves could fall prey to temptation and sin.

It's hard to understand sometimes how a person can stand in a pulpit and preach until the hair stands up on your arms, and pray for the sick and minister deliverance, and still be in bondage to drugs, alcohol, or perversion. Yet we must remember that no one, no matter how powerful or dynamic or eloquent, is immune to the continual presence and pull of temptation.

So with that kind of thing being made public, now people are saying, "If these great men of God can't resist temptation, nobody can." Then it becomes easy to justify sin by saying what Paul said, "I've been given a thorn in my flesh because of my all-surpassing revelations." When Paul made that statement about his "thorn in the flesh," he was not referring to a besetting sin or moral weakness. He was referring to satanic voices and messages which taunted and tormented his mind. (2 Cor. 12:7.)

Shall We Go On Sinning?

What shall we say, then? Shall we go on sinning so that grace may increase?

Romans 6:1

The word translated *sinning* in this verse is *hamartia* in Greek. It is an athletic term meaning "to miss the mark" or "not to share in the prize." It refers to the running of a race or engaging in anything having to do with time. To sin, in that context, is to get tired of expending the energy, exerting the effort, and exercising the discipline necessary to carry on the competition to its final conclusion. To sin, in that sense, is just to give in and fall short of the goal.

In life, as in sports, there is a line that is drawn, both by conscience and by will. And to fail to cross that line is to fall short, to lose, to sin.

You and I are Christians, yet we are also human beings. We are not of this world, but we are still in this world. How are we going to deal with the natural temptations of the flesh which we will have to face as long as our spirits are housed in a physical body?

There will always be temptation, just as there will always be tribulation. Yet Scripture tells us in James 1:13,14: **When tempted, no one should say, "God is tempting me." For God cannot be tempted by evil, nor does he tempt anyone; but each one is tempted when, by his own evil desire, he is dragged away and enticed.** The *King James Version* reads:

> **Let no man say when he is tempted, I am tempted of God: for God cannot be tempted with evil, neither tempteth he any man:**
>
> **But every man is tempted, when he is drawn away of his own lust, and enticed.**

If you are a Holy Ghost-filled believer, you may well ask, "What lust? I don't have any lust." It's one thing to have lust (desire) and another thing to be drawn away by it. Then you never sin, because the Bible says that lust (desire) is the motivating force behind all sin:

> **Then, after desire** (lust) **has conceived, it gives birth to sin; and sin, when it is full-grown, gives birth to death.**
>
> **James 1:15**

Later in Romans 6:23, Paul also tells us:

> **For the wages of sin is death, but the gift of God
> is eternal life in Christ Jesus our Lord.**

The use of **the wages** means that we have to work for sin. No one practices sin accidentally. He has to plan on it.

It takes "malice of forethought" to practice sin. It takes courage to sin. It takes ambition to sin. Sin requires a certain kind of discipline. Every once in a while we may slip into sin, but generally our sinning is deliberate. The tendency to sin is always there, within, just as it was with Paul.

The wages of sin is death, but the gift of God is eternal life. God gives eternal life. You can't work for it, earn it, or buy it. But what sin gives you, you will work for, and work hard. Actually you become a slave. And most folks would rather work for the wages of sin than to enjoy the favor of God in righteousness.

No Condemnation, No Separation

> **Therefore, there is now no condemnation for those
> who are in Christ Jesus.**
>
> **For I am convinced that neither death nor life,
> neither angels nor demons, neither the present nor the
> future, nor any powers, neither height nor depth, nor
> anything else in all creation, will be able to separate
> us from the love of God that is in Christ Jesus our Lord.**
> **Romans 8:1,38,39**

The eighth chapter of Romans begins with no condemnation and ends with no separation. Nothing will separate us from God's unconditional love. Therefore, because that's true, it means that God is going to love us anyway, no matter what we do.

"He understands and knows my heart. I'm a human being. I'm only human. And like all humans, I'm not perfect. No one is. And God's grace covers all my sin. 'Amazing grace, how sweet the sound.' "

All of that is in our mentality. Here's the problem:

Such thinking makes the whole Church lethargic and powerless. When we confront an evil spirit, the devil brings up all the bad things we've ever done so we don't feel qualified to cast it out or even to deal with it. We begin to compare ourselves with other people who have failed publicly and say, "Well, if they can't overcome sin and evil, I can't either." That has been the devil's tactic from the beginning. Now he has everybody doubting the ability of anybody — including themselves — to live holy in this present world. However, Titus 2:11,12 says:

> **For the grace of God that brings salvation has appeared to all men. It teaches us to say "No" to ungodliness and worldly passions, and to live self-controlled, upright and godly lives in this present age.**

What shall we say then? Shall we go on sinning that grace may abound, that grace may increase?

We Died to Sin

> **By no means! We died to sin; how can we live in it any longer?**
>
> **Romans 6:2**

According to Ron McIntosh, former chaplain at Oral Roberts University, the scientific definition of that word translated died is "to fall out of correspondence with." We fell out of correspondence with our shortcomings, with missing the mark. How can we live any longer in it since we died to sin?

Baptism and Salvation

> **Or don't you know that all of us who were baptized into Christ Jesus were baptized into his death? We were therefore buried with him through baptism into death in order that, just as Christ was raised from the dead through the glory of the Father, we too may live a new life.**
>
> **Romans 6:3,4**

Let's read what the Apostle Peter had to say about water baptism:

> For Christ also hath once suffered for sins, the just for the unjust, that he might bring us to God, being put to death in the flesh, but quickened by the Spirit:
>
> By which also he went and preached unto the spirits in prison;
>
> Which sometime were disobedient, when once the longsuffering of God waited in the days of Noah, while the ark was a preparing, wherein few, that is, eight souls were saved by water.
>
> The like figure whereunto even baptism doth also now save us (not the putting away of the filth of the flesh, but the answer of a good conscience toward God,) by the resurrection of Jesus Christ.
>
> **1 Peter 3:18-21** KJV

Baptism saves us, but not in the sense of the spiritual term. It is not water baptism that saves, but the answer of a good conscience toward God. Baptism does not just wash dirt off a person's body or life. Rather it gives him a clean conscience toward God — by the resurrection of Jesus Christ.

Just as Jesus came out of the grave, so the person being baptized comes out of the water. This act is symbolic of going into death, burying the old man — burying the flesh with its habits, hobbies, and hungers —- and coming up with a whole new man, with an entirely new conscience.

In Romans 12:1,2 (KJV), Paul wrote:

> I beseech you, therefore, brethren, by the mercies of God, that ye present your bodies a living sacrifice, holy, acceptable unto God, which is your reasonable [a better translation is "spiritual"] **service** [or worship].
>
> And be not conformed to this world, but be ye transformed....

When you are saved (born anew), your spiritual form is changed. You are transformed. You change your form, your "genes." Your genetic makeup changes when you are born again. The Greek word for this birth process is *gennao*, from which we get the word *genetics*. You are re*gene*rated.

And the dominate chromosome in your genes makes your life right.

Biologically, you have both male and female chromosomes, but one dominates the other, which makes you either a male or female.

Spiritually, when you get regenerated you have within you both "chromosomes." You have a "gene" within you that wants to sin, but since you've been regenerated, the dominant chromosome in your spirit makes you want to live right. And the Bible says that sin no longer has mastery over you.

The meaning of one's life is determined by the power or force that rules it. The devil rules dictatorially, tyrannically; the Holy Ghost governs. The Holy Spirit is not a dictator. He never robs you of your choice. He never forces you to do anything you don't want to do.

The devil rules you. He dictates to you and you become his slave. You work for him, and he whips and drives you. You become an addict or an alcoholic or a pervert or a mean, ruthless killer. You are demon-possessed. That doesn't mean that everybody who sins is demon-possessed, but the enemy does want all of you.

God wants all of you, too, but He is a gentleman. When you give your life to Him, He will govern it. He will guide you and lead you and work with you. So when you get baptized in water, it washes your conscience. You have a different "conscientiousness." Your attitude changes.

Slaves and Masters

Teach slaves to be subject to their masters in everything, to try to please them, not to talk back to them, and not to steal from them, but to show that they can be fully trusted, so that in every way they will make the teaching about God our Savior attractive.
Titus 2:9,10

At the time Paul wrote these words, much of the Christian population was a slave. There were a few rich people, and they all had servants. Every servant was a slave, in the sense that they were all menial workers and subservients. They worked in homes or on farms, for large landowners. So almost everybody was considered a slave or employee as opposed to an employer.

Paul's message was, "If you are an employee, be subject to your employer." That's all Paul was saying. He was not giving credibility to slavery. But in the broader spiritual sense of the term, we're slaves either to righteousness or to sin. That's why Paul told Titus to teach slaves to be subject to their masters.

If the devil is your master, you're subject to him. You're going to do what he tells you to do.

Many times young people start off smoking marijuana just for fun. They engage in social drinking, just to be accepted. It's benign. But after a while, that thing gets hold of them, and they can't stop. They lose control over their own bodies, their own physical appetites and wills.

Paul told Titus to teach slaves to be subject to their masters in everything, to try to please them, not to talk back to them. It was part of their witness.

If you're a sinner, it's hard to talk back to the devil. He tells you what to do, and you do it.

Paul also says to teach slaves not to steal from their masters but to show that they can be fully trusted. He means that in the literal sense, but I'm tying it to the next part of that passage.

Saying No to Temptation

For the grace of God that brings salvation has appeared to all men. It teaches us to say "No" to ungodliness and worldly passions, and to live self-controlled, upright and godly lives in this present age.
Titus 2:11,12

The grace of God teaches us, but the Holy Ghost empowers us. The Holy Ghost trains us to say no. The grace teaches us the concept of saying no.

We've got to go beyond the teachings of grace and get into the power teachings where we are trained and disciplined to resist the devil.

I believe that Adam was born initially innocent but not necessarily virtuous. Innocence is a state that a person is in before he knows the difference between right and wrong. Virtue is coming face to face with temptation and resisting the evil for the good. That's where Adam failed.

The grace of God teaches us to live self-controlled, upright and godly lives in this present age.

You may ask, "What are you talking about? You mean I can live a godly upright life today with all that is going on around me?"

This world is not our home. We're just pilgrims and strangers passing through. The enemy is always attacking our fortifications. So when you are assaulted by the devil, don't be discouraged. When you're tempted, don't be alarmed. That is a normal part of Satan's bait, his ammunition.

Just make sure you have the wherewithal to resist that temptation. You've got to make up your mind. It's not just praying, not just reading the Word, not just any one thing. It's all of it together. You must make up your mind in your own transformed will: "I will not become a slave to the passions of my flesh."

A Purified People

While we wait for the blessed hope — the glorious appearing of our great God and Savior, Jesus Christ, who gave himself for us to redeem us from all wickedness and to purify for himself a people that are his very own, eager to do what is good.

Titus 2:13,14

If more preachers would preach along this line regularly during the year, people would have more victory. The Church must learn to take a stand against the devil and his demons and devices. It must teach its people to have a warlike attitude and stance, to resist the devil in full assurance that if they will do so, he will flee from them. (James 4:7.)

The Bible says that he who has suffered in his body has ceased to sin. (1 Pet. 4:1.) I'm so busy exercising my ministry, in overcoming Satan and his snares, I don't have time to sin. I'm so thankful I've got so much to do. It keeps me busy for the Lord and unavailable to the devil who would love to tempt me into sin.

Maybe you think that a person can be so full of the Holy Ghost that he becomes blind to all temptation. That is not true. We must face reality. We are all human beings. We have to bring our body into subjection to the Holy Ghost.

We need to be honest with ourselves. That's why so many fail, flounder, and fall because the Bible says, If you think you're standing strong, watch yourself. (1 Cor. 10:12.) The greatest battle you'll ever face is right after some great spiritual experience.

Elijah was on the mountaintop calling down fire from heaven, making fun of the prophets of Asherah and Baal, laughing at them. Hundreds of them died. He was as bold and fearless as a lion. But right after that, he ran from one woman with terror on his heels. He ran from Jezebel whose name means "unharnessed" or "unhusbanded." The great valiant prophet of the Lord called down fire from heaven and overcame hundreds of heathen adversaries, but then ran like a scared rabbit from Queen Jezebel. (1 Kings 18,19.)

You have to be careful after a mountaintop experience. Never let down your guard. Holiness takes no vacation, not even in the lazy, crazy, hazy days of summer.

I don't know what I would be if I weren't saved, called to preach and disciplined by the Holy Ghost — my single life filled up with the ministry of the Lord Jesus. I'm glad I have a full-time ministry. I'm honest enough to admit that if I weren't preaching, I'd probably go to church and be an ordinary Christian and do all the things most other believers do, but I don't know what level of consecration I'd have.

Be careful what you do with your spare time. The tendency is to get careless and relaxed and to fall into temptation. Paul has a warning note about those leisure-time activities that seem so innocent at the beginning but which can lead to sin and destruction.

Permissible But Not Beneficial

"Everything is permissible for me" — but not everything is beneficial. "Everything is permissible for me" — but I will not be mastered by anything.

1 Corinthians 6:12

The *King James Version* says that all things are lawful, but not all things are expedient. We must be careful with that statement. Let me explain what Paul is saying here.

"Everything is permissible for me," says Paul, "but not everything is advantageous, beneficial, or profitable. Everything is lawful for me, but I will not be mastered or dominated by anything, even if it is lawful."

Paul said, "To the pure, all things are pure." (Rom. 14:20.) That means that since I am pure, I can do just about anything and still not be in sin. I can drink alcoholic beverages and not be in violation of God's law. I can't tell you anywhere in the Scriptures where it says that it is a sin to have a daiquiri or a pina colada. I can tell you once where it says, "Take a little wine for your stomach's sake." (1 Tim. 5:23.)

But despite the legality of drinking, I don't drink. In fact, I won't even sip a non-alcoholic beverage from a glass that looks like it is a wine or cocktail glass — because I want to shun even the appearance of wrongdoing. I don't want to be a stumbling block to anybody. So I just take a Coke — or better yet, orange juice, so I can have something healthy.

Now you might not really prefer orange juice to a cocktail. And it might be perfectly legal for you to have one. But I won't do that because I don't want to take the chance of offending anyone else. So although it is legal for me to drink, it is not expedient, not beneficial, not advantageous. That is what Paul is saying here in this passage.

Food and Sex

"Food for the stomach and the stomach for food" — but God will destroy them both. The body is not meant for sexual immorality, but for the Lord, and the Lord for the body.

1 Corinthians 6:13

Why is it that Paul so often refers to sins involving food and sex? Because those are two driving passions of the human body.

The first sin came into this world through the eyes and the lips. The Bible says that Eve looked at the tree and saw that it was pleasing to the eye (John calls it the lust of the eyes). It was desirable for food (lust of the flesh). It was desirable for gaining wisdom (the pride of life).

Lust of the flesh, lust of the eyes, pride of life. (1 John 2:16.) The first recorded temptation of Christ involved food. "If You are the Son of God, turn these stones into bread." Lust of the flesh. The second temptation was lust of the eyes: "Let me show You the kingdoms of the world; I'll give them to You if You will worship me." The pride of life was expressed in the temptation, "Cast Your body down from the temple and let the angels catch You." (Luke 4:1-12.)

Have you ever noticed how appealing television food commercials are? They make everything look incredibly delicious. Cold, crisp, hard apples. Soft, creamy ice cream. Crispy, golden fried chicken. Bouncing, fluffy, cloud-like biscuits. "Taste them, teeth them, tongue them, roll them around in your mouth. Feel them, think about them." It's all very sensual. The word *sensual* comes from the senses: "See it, hear it, smell it, touch it, taste it."

That's the way the enemy works. He comes to us on the level of our senses, and it's very appealing. It is easy to be led astray, one step at a time. There is something incredibly pleasurable about sin. It is fun. It appeals to the emotions. It is intriguing. It makes us feel like we're getting away with something, putting something over on somebody. And it gets easier each time. Until, like drugs, it becomes an addiction — then it's too late to do anything except make excuses, to claim that "everybody's doing it," to take pride in the fact that at least we are not hypocritical about our "little shortcomings."

Sin appeals to our lower nature — our body, our flesh. It is also deadly. It leads to destruction. That's why we must be on our guard against it.

Avoid Prostitution

By his power God raised the Lord from the dead, and he will raise us also. Do you not know that your bodies are members of Christ himself? Shall I then take the members of Christ and unite them with a prostitute? Never! Do you not know that he who unites himself with a prostitute is one with her in body? For it is said, "The two will become one flesh." But he who unites himself with the Lord is one with him in spirit.

1 Corinthians 6:14-17

A prostitute is not just some woman standing around on the street corner wearing a tight miniskirt. There are a lot of other prostitutes in life that don't look like women. Prostitution may not be sexual. It may be emotional. It may be mental. It may be financial. It is possible to prostitute oneself in many ways. Our first love is Jesus Christ, and when we indulge in self-seeking pleasure of any kind outside that relationship, we are involved in prostitution. Instead of uniting our bodies with harlots, we are to unite our spirits with Christ.

Honor God With Your Physical Body

Flee from sexual immorality. All other sins a man commits are outside his body, but he who sins sexually sins against his own body. Do you not know that your body is a temple of the Holy Spirit, who is in you,

**whom you have received from God? You are not your
own; you were bought at a price. Therefore honor God
with your body.**

1 Corinthians 6:18-20

If this message were preached regularly in the churches
of America, it would save families, marriages, teenagers.
It may make some people uncomfortable, but it is God trying
to tell all of us something.

Let us heed this word from the Lord. Let us not
continue sinning just because grace abounds. We must learn
to say no to our lower nature — to the gravity of sin which
pulls us down to death and destruction — and say yes to
our higher nature, the grace of God which calls us to live
above and beyond all that we can ask or imagine.

12
Though It Linger, Wait

The oracle that Habakkuk the prophet received.
Habakkuk 1:1

Habakkuk is an Old Testament prophet. His name means "embrace," or some theologians say it is the name of a plant. We don't know much about this prophet. His entire book is only three chapters long. We do know that he was a contemporary of Jeremiah and is categorized as a "minor prophet."

Jeremiah, Ezekiel, Daniel, and Isaiah were considered major prophets because they did major works. Most of their ministries lasted anywhere from thirty to forty years or longer. Habakkuk did not have a long ministry. At least not judging by the words of his book.

He seemed quite agitated in his writing. In fact, his book actually opens with a complaint. He is concerned about his future in God and the future of his people, Israel.

In a previous chapter I wrote about destiny and hope and how they relate. I examined the word *determination,* which is another way to define the will of God. There is the perfect will of God, then there is the permissive will of God. The perfect will of God is God's determined resolve. It is something that is absolutely going to happen with or without us. Then there is the area called the permissive will which involves God's gracious design. There is room for flexibility within that sphere.

Most of us spend our time in the permissive will, passing in and out of the perfect will. Even when we are in the perfect will of God, we don't always know it because the perfect will of God for us is not always what we think it should be. And the perfect will of God is affected by the imperfect will. That's just the way life is. Life is full of questions, many of which will never be answered. And the world is full of right answers to wrong questions.

As we examine the book of Habakkuk, I want to deal with where we are in the Body of Christ. I want to examine where we stand and who we are in Jesus. Of course, I'm reflecting on my own position in the world. I care about who I am in Christ and what role I play in God's master plan.

God has a scheme and tactic — a *modus operandi*. He has a certain system of procedural behaviors in which we must all participate and to which we must submit. In fact, in many ways we do so automatically whether we know it or not. But we participate in it better if we are conscious of it. We need to think destiny. We need to think significance.

None of us is insignificant. No human being is. Or at least no human being is designed to be. Many are living insignificant lives because of ignorance. But I want you to feel that you are an integral part of the vitality of God, of the procreation of heaven, of the expansion of the things of the Lord. If you can grasp this concept, when you wake up every morning your whole perspective on life and yourself will be dramatically changed.

I want to talk about a man who was very vexed by conditions as he saw them and sought God for explanations, for answers to some of his questions. Remember, he is not a man who doesn't have faith. He is a man called of God and anointed of God. He is a prophet. Who of us has not been perplexed by events that challenge our understanding of the character and nature of God? Who do you know who has not wanted at times to bring these questions to God Himself and say to the Lord, "Give me some clarification; my problems don't make sense; my circumstances seem inconsistent with what I know about You; I cannot reconcile this situation with Your faithfulness"? And on and on.

Like Habakkuk, I am a man of God and a preacher of the Gospel who carries a certain burden. Habakkuk called himself an oracle of God. The *King James Version* translates this beginning verse: **The burden which Habakkuk the** prophet did see. This word *burden* refers to something that is lifted or held up, something that is carried. Every Christian is carrying something, though he may not understand its worth. All he knows is that it is heavy. That heaviness sometimes intimidates his faith and challenges his understanding.

As we have seen, the word *destined* means "to be marked out" or "to have limits or boundaries." It implies being secure within those boundaries because nothing can penetrate them or exit from them that is not allowed of God. The Lord has destined, or predestined, you and me to certain determined resolves, and settled conclusions.

Tomorrow has always been an elusive thing to me, and I'm sure you would say the same for yourself. It's hard to get a grasp on tomorrow. It always seems so far away. And yet we must believe in tomorrow because we were here yesterday. So there's always hope in tomorrow. And hope is not an illusionary thing. It is real. But it is based upon faith.

So I am thinking that there has got to be hope for the situation that we're facing in the world and the Church; otherwise, we should just throw in the towel and forget it. However, there is a price to be paid for believing. There is a price for being sustained and for lasting or surviving these times. There is a price for even having faith. If you didn't have faith in the thing God has called you to do, you would have backed away from it a long time ago. There is a flicker of hope in all of us that keeps us motivated. Even though we've miscarried some dreams and visions, we still believe that when that baby we miscarried moves out of the womb, it makes room for another one who will be healthier and able to live.

So God does have a plan for us, though it is not always clear. Destiny is often confusing when the will of God is unclear. This is what the prophet Habakkuk was dealing with. That is the oracle or the burden that Habakkuk the prophet received. Notice how he saw it. He starts with a complaint. He's not prophesying horizontally, he's complaining vertically.

No Fair!

> **How long, O Lord, must I call for help, but you do not listen? Or cry out to you, "Violence!" but you do not save?**
>
> Habakkuk 1:2

Have you ever been in this situation? Have you ever felt like complaining to God, "Unfair!"? Have you ever cried out, "How long, O Lord, must I call for help, but You do not listen? How long must I cry out to You, 'Unfair! Violation!' and still You don't deliver or rescue or protect or save me"?

If so, you understand the feelings of this unhappy and confused prophet of the Lord.

Why, Lord?

> **Why do you make me look at injustice? Why do you tolerate wrong? Destruction and violence are before me; there is strife, and conflict abounds.**
>
> **Therefore the law is paralyzed, and justice never prevails. The wicked hem in the righteous, so that justice is perverted.**
>
> Habakkuk 1:3,4

"Why do you make me look at injustice?" asks Habakkuk. Instead of *injustice,* the *King James Version* uses the word *iniquity.* Habakkuk is complaining of a lack of equality, a lack of fairness.

"Why do You tolerate wrong?" he wants to know. "Why do You put up with evil? Why do You tolerate things that cause grief?"

"Destruction and violence are before me," he complains. "There is strife everywhere, and conflict abounds." In other words, he is saying, "The law is paralyzed, it's ineffective, it's immobilized, it's nonfunctional; therefore, justice never prevails. It never overrules or overcomes. It doesn't win. Righteousness just doesn't pay! The wicked hem in the righteous, and justice is always perverted.''

Habakkuk is quite upset. He has problems. He asks some hard questions of the Lord. As a result of this man's dialogue with God in which he openly and honestly expresses his doubts and perplexities with strong faith, God gives him some answers.

Sometimes we must ask a few questions — even of God. At times we must feel enough vexation to say, ''Lord, what in the world is going on here? Give me some kind of clarity. Shall I pursue this thing or not? Should I keep on preaching or not? Can we change this situation or not?''

Many of us are really trying to change the whole world singlehandedly. That we cannot do. But we can change our own world, and we can affect the people we come in contact with on a daily basis.

Why do we even go to church? Why do we preach? Why do we endure the things we have to put up with? What's the end of all of this singing and going to choir rehearsals and studying the Scriptures and making notes in our Bible? Is there any point to it all? Are we really accomplishing anything?

That's what Habakkuk is saying to the Lord here in this passage. He is talking to God about the invasion of Judah. He is tired of his people being under the domination of the Babylonians. (They're called the Chaldeans here, but they're really the Babylonians.)

Jeremiah had prophesied for forty years, and the people didn't heed his word. So the Babylonians came and took over Israel, and now they are invading Judah. So Habakkuk makes his complaint, and then God answers.

Look and Be Amazed

Look at the nations and watch — and be utterly amazed. For I am going to do something in your days

that you would not believe, even if you were told.
Habakkuk 1:5

Sometimes God doesn't tell us His plan because we wouldn't believe it anyway. To Habakkuk He says, "Just go on and worry if that's what you want to do. I know what the end is going to be. I've already ordained a resolved conclusion. I would have told you what it was, but you have been so busy complaining that I couldn't. You wouldn't have believed it, even if I had told you, because you're so negative in your attitude."

This Is My Doing

I am raising up the Babylonians, that ruthless and impetuous people, who sweep across the whole earth to seize dwelling places not their own.

They are a feared and dreaded people; they are a law to themselves and promote their own honor.

Their horses are swifter than leopards, fiercer than wolves at dusk. Their cavalry gallops headlong; their horsemen come from afar. They fly like a vulture swooping to devour; they all come bent on violence.

Their hordes advance like a desert wind and gather prisoners like sand.

They deride kings and scoff at rulers. They laugh at all fortified cities; they build earthen ramps and capture them.

Then they sweep past like the wind and go on — guilty men, whose own strength is their god.
Habakkuk 1:6-11

"So you think you're the only one who knows what's going on, Habakkuk," says the Lord. "Well, let me just describe your problem to you."

Sometimes we pray thinking that we are God's secret informants on earth and that without our dramatic descriptions in prayer, He would not know our earthly problems. In this passage God shows the prophet that not only is He absolutely aware of the problem, but that He is

178

actually orchestrating the matter to ultimately accomplish His divine and higher purposes for Israel. He seems to be saying, "I'm going to be Your therapist, and I'm not going to charge you anything but faith. For I'm going to do something in your days that you would not believe even if it were told you. I am raising up this problem."

"What do You mean, Lord? You are the One doing this?" the prophet is thinking.

"Yes," says God, "I am raising up the Babylonians, that ruthless people to come in and loot, devour, steal, destroy and take prisoner. So just relax. I know what I'm doing and why."

Then Habakkuk raises his second complaint.

Why Are You Doing This to Us?

O Lord, are you not from everlasting? My God, my Holy One, we will not die. O Lord, you have appointed them to execute judgment; O Rock, you have ordained them to punish.

Your eyes are too pure to look on evil; you cannot tolerate wrong. Why then do you tolerate the treacherous? Why are you silent while the wicked swallow up those more righteous than themselves?
Habakkuk 1:12,13

"Oh, Lord, couldn't You think of another way to do this? You have ordained that our enemies punish us. Why are You silent while the wicked swallow up those more righteous than they are?" In other words, "We're bad, Lord, but we're not that bad!"

Why Do the Wicked Prosper?

You have made men like fish in the sea, like sea creatures that have no ruler.

The wicked foe pulls all of them up with hooks, he catches them in his net, he gathers them up in his dragnet; and so he rejoices and is glad.

> **Therefore he sacrifices to his net and burns incense to his dragnet, for by his net he lives in luxury and enjoys the choicest food.**
>
> Habakkuk 1:14-16

In modern times I would be saying: "The evil man worships what he does and sacrifices to and for it. Drug pushers are making millions of dollars and enjoying the choicest lifestyles. They're eating steak and lobster while I eat hamburgers and fries. Is this right, Lord? Is this fair?"

How Long Will This Go On?

> **Is he to keep on emptying his net, destroying nations without mercy?**
>
> Habakkuk 1:17

"How long is this going to go on? The drug lord lives better than I do. He drives a better car than I do. He wears better clothes than I do. He lives in a 5,000-square-foot home, and I'm barely able to pay for my two-bedroom apartment.

"And I'm the one who is saved. I'm the one who has 'faith' stickers hanging on the refrigerator and stuck on the car bumper. I'm the one who is standing and confessing and believing. I'm the one who has 'I am the Lord that healeth thee' stuck on my medicine cabinet."

It's like, "Hey, God, what's the big deal here?"

This is a valid concern of a man who has legitimate questions.

Lord, What Do You Have To Say?

> **I will stand at my watch and station myself on the ramparts; I will look to see what he will say to me, and what answer I am to give to this complaint** [or, what to answer when I am rebuked].
>
> Habakkuk 2:1

"I will wait to see what I will answer when I get rebuked. You can strike me down if You want to, Lord, but I don't like the way things are. I don't understand what

You are doing. I've got to have some answers, even if it means getting in trouble with You.

"I've got to voice my complaint, my lamentation, and cry out from my heart and tell You what's really in my soul. I feel that You've called me and anointed me, but I don't see enough evidence, Lord. You've got to do something about this situation."

Now watch the Lord. My friend, get ready, buckle your seat belt. God is about to answer.

The Lord's Answer

Then the Lord replied:

"Write down the revelation and make it plain on tablets so that a herald may run with it.

For the revelation awaits an appointed time; it speaks of the end and will not prove false. Though it linger, wait for it; it will certainly come and will not delay."

Habakkuk 2:2,3

The clarity, the unveiling, the uncovering awaits an appointed time. It speaks of the conclusion. It speaks of the end and will not prove false. Though it may seem to delay in appearing, wait for it.

An answer is coming. A revelation is on its way. It speaks of a conclusion. God wrote the book. He knows the ending. There's always something about our problem that we don't know and only God knows because God really has no problems. All He has are solutions. God doesn't have any questions. All He has are answers. So He is demanding that we trust Him in situations we don't understand.

The Just Shall Live by Faith

See, he is puffed up; his desires are not upright — but the righteous will live by his faith — indeed, wine betrays him; he is arrogant and never at rest.

> Because he is as greedy as the grave and like death
> is never satisfied, he gathers to himself all the nations
> and takes captive all the peoples.
>
> Habakkuk 2:4,5

The enemy is full of self-sufficient arrogance. His desires are not upright. But the righteous — the *King James Version* says "the just" — will live by faith.

The just, the righteous, are those who are in right standing or right posture or right position with God. These will live by their faith. That word *faith* is not like the one used in the New Testament. To have faith in the Old Testament meant to be firm, to be secure. So the just will live by their own fidelity, security, steadfastness, and firmness.

We cannot, and we must not, allow circumstances to upset our security system. We must remain firm and unintimidated by anything that happens to us or goes on around us.

In the face of questions and misunderstandings and misinterpretations and misgivings, we must be destined, determined people. The righteous person, the one who is in right standing, the one who has been positioned and poised by God, just stands there — regardless of outward circumstances or inward emotions. Like Habakkuk, we must take our stand and then wait faithfully until the answer comes.

Wait for the Lord

Notice this passage in Psalm 27:

> The Lord is my light and my salvation — whom shall I fear? The Lord is the stronghold of my life — of whom shall I be afraid?
>
> When evil men advance against me to devour my flesh, when my enemies and my foes attack me, they will stumble and fall. [When they slander me, they won't have a leg to stand on.]

182

> **Though an army besiege me, my heart will not fear; though war break out against me, even then will I be confident.**
>
> **I am still confident of this: I will see the goodness of the Lord in the land of the living.**
>
> **Wait for the Lord; be strong and take heart and wait for the Lord.**
>
> **Psalm 27:1-3,13,14**

The *King James Version* of verse 13 says, **I had fainted, unless I had believed to see the goodness of the Lord in the land of the living.**

I would faint, give up, if I did not see the goodness of the Lord somewhere. If I didn't see that there was a positive conclusion to this situation we are facing today, I would have fainted and quit a long time ago. But I am confident of one thing: I am going to see some goodness. I refuse to see only defeat. I will not be a negative person. I will stand firm in my faith.

In Verse 14 the psalmist tells us to wait on the Lord, to be strong and take heart and wait. In Hebrew the word translated *wait* means "to bind together by twisting."

Collect yourself in a cord or rope or line or linen. The word *linen* is a derivative of the word *line*. In other words, weave yourself to God. Get wrapped up and tied up, wrapped around and twisted up in faith that sustains and protects us.

According to Romans 8, our destiny is determined by God, so we should not fear any unanswerable questions. All the days of our appointed time we should wait upon the Lord, wait until our answer comes.

Soar on Wings of Eagles

> **Even youths grow tired and weary, and young men stumble and fall; but those who hope in the Lord [the King James Version says "wait on the Lord"] will renew their strength.**

> **They will soar on wings like eagles; they will run
> and not grow weary, they will walk and not be faint.**
>
> **Isaiah 40:30,31**

If you wait on the Lord, if your hope is in the Lord, you are not going to faint; you're going to soar on wings like an eagle. When your hope is in the Lord, you will ''mount up'' as the *King James Version* says. You will start ascending. The more you hope in the Lord, the higher you rise.

You're not going to be intimidated by the circumstances, not even intimidated by things you don't know or understand. Even though you've erred and made mistakes, you're still called of the Lord, and somehow everything is going to work out right.

Trust in the Lord

> **Fret not thyself because of evildoers, neither be
> thou envious against the workers of iniquity.**
>
> **For they shall soon be cut down like the grass, and
> wither as the green herb.**
>
> **Trust in the Lord, and do good; so shalt thou dwell
> in the land, and verily thou shalt be fed.**
>
> **Psalm 37:1-3 KJV**

The way you dwell in the land is by trusting in the Lord. Do good — which means, do what is right — and trust God.

I'm going to dwell in that land. I'm going to stand in that land. I'm going to abide in that land. I'm not going to run away. I'm digging in my heels to maintain residence in the will of God.

Delight in the Lord

> **Delight thyself also in the Lord; and he shall give
> thee the desires of thine heart.**
>
> **Psalm 37:4 KJV**

To delight means to make yourself attractive to God. Do the things that get His attention. Make yourself desirable to the Lord, and He will give you the right desires, God desires, in your heart. Then He will grant them.

Commit Your Way to God

Commit thy way unto the Lord; trust also in him; and he shall bring it to pass.

Psalm 37:5 KJV

Commit everything to the Lord, trust Him, and rest in His peace.

I believe we're going to emerge victorious. I believe that the revival we're anticipating is already in the birth canal. It's moving on down. It's about to be brought forth. But we must be patient and strong in waiting.

An old Negro spiritual I used to hear when I was a boy said, "You can't hurry God, oh no, you just gotta wait. You gotta trust Him and give Him time, no matter how long He takes. He's God, and He don't hurry. He'll be there, don't you worry. He may not come when you want Him to, but He's right on time."

At the tomb of Lazarus, Jesus was four days late in arriving. But as soon as He got there, Lazarus came out. So don't envy those who are unrighteous, who appear to be succeeding in their evil. Don't worry about those who are coming against you and slandering you for righteousness' sake. In the end you will see the victory of the Lord, and so will they.

Wait Patiently and Joyfully

I heard and my heart pounded, my lips quivered at the sound; decay crept into my bones, and my legs trembled. Yet I will wait patiently for the day of calamity to come on the nation invading us.

Though the fig tree does not bud and there are no grapes on the vines, though the olive crop fails and the fields produce no food, though there are no sheep in the pen and no cattle in the stalls, yet I will rejoice in the Lord, I will be joyful in God my Savior.

The Sovereign Lord is my strength; he makes my feet like the feet of a deer, he enables me to go on the heights.

Habakkuk 3:16-19

Have the faith and confidence of Habakkuk. Be patient and stand firm. Rejoice in the Lord your God, the Source of your strength, knowing that in the end the enemy will be defeated, and righteousness will once again prevail!

13
Our Time Has Come

Until now you have not asked for anything in my name. Ask and you will receive, and your joy will be complete.

John 16:24

This scene took place just a short time before Jesus was to be taken from His disciples and His earthly work.

"Up to this point," Jesus said, "you have never asked anything in My name." He did not say that they had not asked anything. He said that they had not asked anything *in His name*. This doesn't just mean His title, it refers to His character, His authority.

"You haven't asked anything in My purpose," Jesus is saying. "You haven't asked anything in the spirit of My calling. You have been asking for things, plenty of things. Too many things. But you haven't asked for them in the right spirit. You haven't asked for the right reasons, out of the right motivation."

Hitherto you and I have asked nothing in the name of Jesus. But now that things are changing, now that our new and fresh anointing is coming, we're going to begin to ask differently. Now we're going to begin to pray in the Holy Ghost. We're going to begin to ask things that God already has in store for us. Our prayers and requests are now going to be in the will of God.

Our Time Has Come

In this passage, Jesus is just days away from Calvary. He is warning His disciples that His days on earth are numbered, that He is about to be taken from them. But He promises to send back to them the Holy Ghost.

I was born again when I was five years old. During the years since that time, I have grown in the Lord. But even at that early age, I had a grasp on Jesus and on His will for me. I was absolutely sure then that I was called to preach the Gospel.

Now I understand that all the years up to this point in my life have been preparatory for this moment. Generally a man doesn't get a clear understanding of who he is until somewhere between the ages of thirty-five and forty-five. He grows and goes through trials and tests as he is involved in many different experiences of life. Then when he begins to approach forty years of age — as I am now at the time of this writing — he begins to get a firmer grasp of who he is. He starts coming into some form of maturity and self-actualization.

My particular generation, which is just beginning to emerge, is succeeding a generation which will be going home to God within the next decade or two. Had I turned forty a decade earlier, those we have been leaning on for the last thirty or forty years would have still been in their prime. But now many of those great men and women of God are being called home to their rewards. I'm not announcing their death or pronouncing their departure. Some of them will be here another twenty years or so. But when they are taken from us, another crop of young men and women full of the Spirit of Jesus will come on the world scene with a double anointing of the last generation plus their own.

I believe that I am in that number, and that you are, too. I believe that we are called and chosen and equipped of God to touch the whole nation and world with the Gospel. I have faith in my heart that I have never felt before. I have a courage that I have never known. I have ambition I have never experienced. I have divine inclinations that are totally new to me. I feel I am a different person. I feel I am coming into my spiritual realm. I'm not boasting. I'm simply telling you what I'm feeling deep down in my spirit.

One of my divine calls in life is to remind my generation that there is hope for the future. I know statistics say there isn't. I know the situation in our country — financially, morally, and spiritually — looks bleak. But it's because the voice of the prophet has not been heard. But God is raising up a prophetic, apostolic, pastoral, evangelistic word, a word that people are going to have to listen to, whether they like it or not, because there's a new outpouring of power and authority that's coming with that word.

I apologize if I sound arrogant because I don't mean to, but I do mean to sound confident, full of conviction, full of divine intuition, full of the flame and faith and fire of God in my soul.

Hitherto I have not asked things as I'm about to ask them. I have not understood how to ask. I have not had the inclination to ask. I'm taking this word personally for my own life and for my own ministry. And for you who are reading these words right now, God has a word for you from heaven.

God is saying to this generation, ''Arise and shine, for your light has come and the glory of the Lord is upon you. I want you to feel good about everything. I want you to feel positive about everything. I want you to feel reinforcement and faith for everything.''

Nothing the devil throws at us is going to work. It's going to be like water on a duck's back because our time has come.

When Jesus' time came, He walked through a hostile crowd that wanted to throw Him off the brow of a hill. But the Bible says that He turned and walked right through them, and nobody interfered with Him. (Luke 4:28-30.) When your time has come, you can go through the most adverse situations. You can go through the most trying times. There are periods when the devil just can't have any affect on you. There are seasons in your life when God just lets everything bloom like springtime. And no chill can keep the seed under the soil. No storm can stop it from rising to its own maturity.

I feel that my time has come, that no weapon formed against me can prosper because it's not by might, nor by power, but it's by the Spirit of the Lord. (Zech. 4:6.) Greater is He Who is within me than he who is in the world. (1 John 4:4.) I've got power in my life. Don't you?

I have given notice to the devil that my time has come to destroy his works and to cast him out of my mind — and my world. That should be your outlook, your testimony and your experience, because your time has also come.

The Spirit of Truth

"When the Counselor comes, whom I will send to you from the Father, the Spirit of truth who goes out from the Father, he will testify about me; but you also must testify, for you have been with me from the beginning."

John 15:26

Jesus tells His disciples that He is sending to them the Counselor, the Comforter, the Advocate or Intercessor, the Spirit of truth. The Greek word translated *Spirit* here is *pneuma*, meaning "wind" or "breath." The word *truth* actually means "clarity, that which is no longer concealed."

The Lord is sending upon us a fresh revelation of the Spirit of wisdom and understanding.

Be on Your Guard

"All this I have told you so that you will not go astray."

John 16:1

The Greek word translated "go astray" in this passage is *skandalizo*, which the *King James Version* translates as "be offended." It also means "be entrapped, tripped up, or enticed." Jesus was preparing His disciples so they would not be misled, offended, or scandalized. I don't know about you, but I am tired of scandals.

"I'm telling you this," says the Lord, "so you will not be deceived or tricked or entrapped or led away or led astray. So that you will not be enticed to sin. So that you will not backslide or miss the target."

There is a target out in front of us. And Jesus is warning us here that there is trouble ahead, but that in a short while He will be coming to us revealing Himself to us with a fresh touch of wisdom and power.

I Have Warned You

They [the religious people] **will put you out of the synagogue; in fact, a time is coming when anyone who kills you will think he is offering a service to God. They will do such things because they have not known the Father or me. I have told you this, so that when the time comes you will remember that I warned you. I did not tell you this at first because I was with you.**
John 16:2-4

Jesus is informing His disciples that He is going to be removed from them physically. He is warning them ahead of time, ''You're going to have a little hell on your way to heaven.''

Hell means the place where the enemy is in dominance. When the devil comes against your life, he brings hell. Sometimes you may go through difficult times, but always remember: you're on your way to heaven. So Jesus is saying to us here, ''I'm warning you, you're going to have trouble. But don't let that trouble cause you to be entrapped because the pain is just before the promise. The question is just before the answer. The problem precedes the solution.''

I Am Going Away

Now I am going to him who sent me [on this particular mission], **yet none of you asks me, ''Where are you going?'' Because I have said these things, you are filled with grief** [sorrow]. **But I tell you the truth: It is for your good that I am going away. Unless I go away, the Counselor** [the Holy Ghost] **will not come to you; but if I go, I will send him to you. When he comes, he will convict** [or convince or admonish] **the world of guilt in regard to sin** [failure, fault] **and**

191

righteousness [or right standing] **and judgment** [decision or benevolence].

John 16:5-8

Jesus was leaving the earth physically. He told His disciples, who were grieved by His words, that it was better for them that He left because then He would send upon them the Holy Ghost Who would convict (issue a verdict, render a judgment, pronounce sentence upon) the world of sin.

The Prince of This World Is Condemned

In regard to sin, because men do not believe in me [or obey Me]; **in regard to righteousness, because I am going to the Father, where you can see me no longer; and in regard to judgment, because the prince of this world now stands condemned.**

John 16:9-11

The prince of this world — Satan, the devil, the thief, the liar, the murderer, the accuser — is condemned. The devil is already defeated. He is now convicted and sentenced. And we are on the Advocate's side. We are with the Plaintiff against Satan. We have won!

The devil has had his day. Confusion has had its day. Delusion has had its day. Deception has had its day. Now truth will prevail in our lives.

As Spirit-filled and Spirit-led Christians, we are not going to be confused any longer. We are not going to be slipping and sliding any longer. Our time has come.

This may seem fantastic to you, but I actually believe that God is going to anoint us to stop the crime and drugs and violence of our society. I believe that the Church is about to rise like an island in the sea, and a new mantle of authority and power and conviction and courage is going to come upon us.

Many of the people to whom I looked as pastors are gone. Most of my Sunday school teachers who taught me when I was young have gone to heaven. Many of the great men and women of God who have carried the torch for the last thirty or forty years are looking for successors. Their gaze is heavenward, but there is a group of young men and women whom God is raising up to take their places. There's a new authority, a new self-confidence that is coming upon us. We have to be what our elders and leaders are looking for. Our time has come to catch the baton and run with it.

We, God's people, are the ones to whom God is giving the answers, the miracles, the solutions the world is seeking.

Guided Into All Truth

I have much more to say to you, more than you can now bear. But when he, the Spirit of truth, comes, he will guide you into all truth....

John 16:12,13

Truth is not concealing. When the Spirit of truth comes — the Spirit of clearness or clarification or revelation and interpretation — He will lead us into all truth.

He Will Tell You What Is To Come

...He will not speak on his own [or of Himself]; **he will speak only what he hears, and he will tell you what is yet to come.**

John 16:13

In the Greek that word translated *hears* implies that the Holy Spirit will only speak that which He is in audience of. The Holy Spirit is in the presence and audience of both man and God simultaneously. He is hearing from God and discerning man at the same time. And He is communicating what He hears. If we listen to Him, He will tell us what is yet to come.

What Is Mine Is Yours

He will bring glory to me by taking from what is mine and making it known to you.

John 16:14

That phrase *what is mine* means "pertaining to or relating to." It refers to that which proceeds out of the Lord. The Holy Ghost will bring glory to Jesus by taking what pertains to Him, relates to Him, belongs to Him, or proceeds from Him, and making it known or evident and identifiable to the believer.

What Is God's Is Mine

All that belongs to the Father is mine. That is why I said the Spirit will take from what is mine and make it known to you.

John 16:15

Everything that belongs to God somehow relates to Jesus. And He has promised to make it known to us through the Person and ministry of the Holy Spirit.

You Will See Me As I Am

In a little while you will see me no more, and then after a little while you will see me.

John 16:16

The word *see* is used twice in that sentence, but it's used in two different ways in the Greek. The first one is *theoreo*, which relates to our words *theory* and *theoretical*. Its dictionary meaning is "to be a spectator of." Jesus is telling His disciples, "In a while you will be spectators of Me no longer."

That word *spectator* implies the careful perusal of the details of an object. It points especially to the vision of the beholder.

The second time the word *see* appears in this verse, it is the Greek word *optanomai* meaning "to gaze with wide open eyes as at something remarkable."

"Up till now you have been spectators, theorizers, of Me," says the Lord. "But now that's going to change. Soon you're going to actually discern and experience Me, to know Me as I am. You're going to be fascinated at how remarkable

I really am. You've been seeing me obscurely, in the natural, the same way you have been praying.

"Until now you have not asked anything in My name because you didn't know Me. But now you're going to see Me as I am, but not with natural eyes. You're going to see something with your spiritual discernment, and it's going to change your whole way of seeing and asking."

A Great Change Is Coming

Some of his disciples said to one another, "What does he mean by saying, 'In a little while you will see me no more, and then after a little while you will see me,' and 'Because I am going to the Father'?" They kept asking, "What does he mean by 'a little while'? We don't understand what he is saying."

Jesus saw that they wanted to ask him about this, so he said to them, "Are you asking one another what I meant when I said, 'In a little while you will see me no more, and then after a little while you will see me'? I tell you the truth, you will weep and mourn while the world rejoices. You will grieve, but your grief will turn to joy."

John 16:17-20

There is going to be a little more weeping and mourning, because between the beginning of 1992 and the middle of 1993 and throughout this decade, there are going to be a lot of exits, a lot of changes — some dramatic and extraordinary.

Many of us will bury dear and precious loved ones. The strong towers and pillars that we have leaned upon and against for the last forty to fifty years are going to be taken from us. There is coming a changing of the guard. I predict and prophesy that by the middle of 1993, there will be a tremendous conspicuous change in the cosmetic appearance and structure of the Church. A great change is coming.

"I tell you the truth," says the Lord, "you will weep and mourn while the world rejoices." It is going to look as if the world is killing the Church. They are going to try to take away our non-taxable status. They are going to attack top preachers. Other scandals are going to hit. There are other dark secrets that are going to be exposed. The Internal Revenue Service is going to assault us. There's going to be weeping and mourning. This won't last long because weeping only endures for the night, but joy comes in the morning. (Ps. 30:5.)

We will grieve, but in the end our grief will turn to joy.

The Time Has Arrived

A woman giving birth to a child has pain because her time has come; but when her baby is born she forgets the anguish because of her joy that a child is born into the world.

John 16:21

Again, as we've stated earlier, you may be hurting, questioning, overburdened, overweight while you're carrying what is growing within you. But your "baby" will be born. The miracle will be wrought. The answer will come. The revival is on its way. The confusion, the doubt, the questions, the loneliness, the fear, the self-pity; it's all going out the window. God is about to give us clarification.

We Will Rejoice

So with you: Now is your time of grief, but I will see you again and you will rejoice, and no one will take away your joy.

John 16:22

We will see Him again. We will see revival again, hope again, and we will rejoice. And this time the devil won't take it away. No trial, no setback, will take away our joy.

Ask and Receive

In that day you will no longer ask me anything. I tell you the truth, my Father will give you whatever you ask in my name.

John 16:23

In the Greek this word *ask* means "call for, crave, desire, request, or require." Jesus is telling us that if we will call for anything that we require or request or need, we will receive it. That word *receive* means we will be satisfied, crammed full, overfurnished, full to overflowing.

We had better make room because we require a lot.

Fullness of Joy

Until now you have not asked for anything in my name. Ask and you will receive, and your *joy* **will be complete.**

John 16:24

Here the Greek word translated *joy* is chara, meaning "calm delight," or "cheerfulness."

The Bible says that in the Lord's presence there is fullness of joy. (Ps. 16:11.) That means that in His *appearance* or "apparentness" there is fullness of joy. The joy of the Lord is our strength. The Lord's joy, His calm delight and assurance, is our strength. He is so calm, so cool, so collected because He knows exactly what's going on and what the final outcome will be.

He is our source of strength and comfort. As long as our Leader is calm and assured, we followers can be also. As long as the Captain is not sweating and trembling, then there is no need for the crew to be anxious.

God is not worried about a thing. He has everything under control. So don't worry. The joy of the Lord, the calm assurance, the delight, the rejoicing of the Lord, is our stronghold. (Neh. 8:10.) Our strength is in the things that make God happy. And when God is happy, our joy is complete.

Let's begin to ask and receive. But let's be sure to request the things that God wants us to receive.

Something incredible is about to happen. The greatest visitation the Church has ever known is just around the corner. We're about to experience the glory of the Lord.

We're going to walk through hostility as Jesus walked through the angry mob. It's time to stop eating manna and start making the walls of Jericho tumble down. It's time to stop wandering in the wilderness and begin to go from miracles of endurance to miracles of conquest.

In That Day

Though I have been speaking figuratively, a time is coming when I will no longer use this kind of language but will tell you plainly about my Father. In that day you will ask in my name. I am not saying that I will ask the Father on your behalf. No, the Father himself loves you because you have loved me and have believed that I came from God.

John 16:25-27

We are about to be divinely visited with the Spirit of sovereignty. God is going to steer this ship through the high seas of turmoil and change. We are going to experience a new power in our praying so that we will ask the Lord for things we have never felt confident enough to ask Him before. The Spirit of the Lord is saying that our destinies are now about to be fulfilled.

The Lord spoke this to me as I was preparing this message: "Hitherto My people have not asked in My name, in My will, in My spirit. Tell them to ask, that their joy might be complete."

We're going to begin to pray for something, and our prayer is going to go another way — we are going to pray ourselves into the will of God. The Holy Ghost is going to intercede, intervene, and sometimes interfere in order to keep our prayers free from that which doesn't belong in them.

Let's begin to ask, that our joy might be full. We may have to weep for a little while this evening, but joy is coming in the morning!

14
On Our Way

The book of Daniel, especially the last six chapters, has to be one of the most difficult books of the Bible to understand. It is full of eschatological obscurities. Eschatology refers to the study of end times. The books of Daniel, Ezekiel, and Revelation are all books of the apocalypse, that is, the revelation.

A Man of Revelation

Daniel is a very interesting character. The first six chapters of the book which bear his name deal with almost fairy-tale like stories that we learned, most of us, at our mother's knee or in Sunday school when we were children.

We all remember the stories of Daniel in the den of lions; Shadrach, Meshach, and Abednego, the three Hebrew children thrown into the fiery furnace; King Belshazzar and the handwriting on the wall; Daniel and his friends refusing to eat the king's rich fare, choosing instead the healthier foods of the Hebrews; Daniel, under God's anointing, interpreting the dreams of King Nebuchadnezzar, etc.

Daniel and his Hebrew friends were all young men when they entered Babylon some seventy years prior to the writing of this book. Daniel lived to be in his mid-eighties or nineties. But he was a teenager when he was carried away from his homeland to live through the Babylonian captivity.

Though Daniel was a man of revelation, he spent the last portion of his life, the part described in the final six chapters of the book of Daniel, in considerable confusion. He grappled desperately with many "unknowns." When it came to King Nebuchadnezzar's dreams or visions, Daniel could interpret them. But, like us, Daniel had a hard time interpreting his own dreams and visions.

He had no trouble with the den of lions, no trouble with the fiery furnace, no trouble with the handwriting on the wall. He had no trouble refusing to compromise. But he did

have trouble understanding the vision of God for his life
and for Israel.

A Man of Principle

In this prophet, Daniel, we find a timeless
demonstration of separation from impurity. All his life he
refused to compromise his principles. That's what we can
learn from Daniel.

Daniel was also faithful in prayer. He prayed effectual,
fervent prayers. He had uninterrupted, unmitigated
devotion to the Lord God Whose Kingdom is from
generation to generation.

Daniel came along at a time that was pivotal in the
history of the world. World empires were changing, much
as they are today. The communistic empire is crumbling.
Even the position of the United States in the world is being
altered dramatically. The Supreme Court has become more
conservative in the last several years. That conservatism
perhaps will trigger, as a word of prophecy has stated, some
radical differences in our land.

During crisis times in history, people, even sinners and
unbelievers, somehow are unusually interested in
predictions or prophesies about the future. We are facing
a critical time right now, and people are looking to the
future. This is based both on man's natural curiosity and
also on his desire for security and assurance, which many
are not finding in many present, existing agencies. They
are looking for something that will offer some kind of hope
and promise for the future.

The book of Daniel and parts of Ezekiel and Revelation
hold some kind of an odd fascination for modern writers
who are always trying to delineate what these books are
saying. And it's very difficult to know what interpretation
should be accepted as valid. Yet God's eternal truth
concerning His Church, concerning His people, is valid in
any generation. Though it may delay at times, no historical

change is going to hinder or in any way obstruct God's sovereign plan for the world.

A Man With Questions

We are God's people, and there is a divine plan for us — corporately and individually. Daniel had lots of questions and we will deal with some of them in this chapter. He ends the book in Chapter 12, verses 8 through 12, by saying:

> I heard, but I did not understand. So I asked, "My lord, what will the outcome of all this be?"
>
> He replied, "Go your way, Daniel, because the words are closed up and sealed until the time of the end. Many will be purified, made spotless and refined, but the wicked will continue to be wicked. None of the wicked will understand, but those who are wise will understand.
>
> "From the time that the daily sacrifice is abolished and the abomination that causes desolation is set up, there will be 1,290 days. Blessed is the one who waits for and reaches the end of the 1,335 days."

We have said that God has a destiny, a determined end in mind for us, His children. But some of the things that happen prior to that predetermined ending will cause questions, confusion, and bewilderment for us, like that experienced by the great prophet, Daniel.

Often the revelations we are given by the Lord don't make sense. It made very little sense to Daniel, so the Lord told him to go his way because the words were closed up and sealed until the time of the end. Or until God's determination. Then the Lord added these words: "Many will be purified, made spotless and refined." (The word *refined*, or tried, means "to be exacted" or "to be made pure.") "But the wicked will continue to be wicked, no matter what happens. None of the wicked will understand." (They won't get the proposed intentions of God.) "But those who are wise, those who have insight from heaven, those who can look in and get some kind of discernment, those who walk in the Spirit will understand. From the time that the daily sacrifice is abolished and the abomination that causes desolation to set up, there will be 1,290 days.''

This event actually took place historically in the days before Christ.

A Greek leader, Antiochus Epiphanes, took a hog or a pig and sacrificed it on the altar in the holy temple of Jerusalem. That's called the abomination which causes desolation. This event took place shortly after Daniel's writing of this book.

''Blessed is the one who waits and reaches the end.'' You and I are blessed because we will wait and reach the end of the 1,335 days. (This number has natural and historical significance.) But in the meantime, the Lord has a word for us today, just as He did for Daniel then. That word is the message I want to share with you in this chapter.

Go Your Way

As for you, go your way till the end. You will rest, and then at the end of the days you will rise to receive your allotted inheritance.

Daniel 12:13

As for you and me, we are on our way. We will not stop. We will not give in. We will not give up. We will not give out. We're going all the way. We are going to see what the end will be like.

The book of Daniel, as we have seen, ends with dreams and visions and their interpretation. Like us today, Daniel didn't have a lot of clarity about the future, but he understood where he was at the moment. We must live, we must die, and we must live until we die and then as Christians we will live again.

Two Kinds of Faith

The vision of the evenings and mornings that has been given you is true, but seal up the vision, for it concerns the distant future.

Daniel 8:26

I believe there are two kinds of faith: telescopic and microscopic. Telescopic faith takes the distant future and brings it close. Microscopic faith takes that which is close and amplifies it, magnifies it, to produce clarity.

In this eighth chapter the Lord tells Daniel that the vision he has received is true, but that he should seal it up and preserve it, because it is telescopic — it concerns the far distant future.

Get Up and Go About the King's Business

I, Daniel, was exhausted and lay ill for several days. Then I got up and went about the king's business. I was appalled [astonished, confused, astounded] **by the vision; it was beyond understanding.**

Daniel 8:27

There are a lot of folks who see visions but have no understanding of their immediate or future meaning. It's one thing to see a vision and another thing to have a vision. What you have, you don't necessarily see visually. You have it. It's a part of you. You're going about carrying out the vision that you don't see outwardly. You're walking by faith and not by what you perceive with the natural eye or senses.

You are a child of destiny. God is orchestrating and ordaining your steps and your life — if you are yielded to Him. All yielded vessels have visions whether they see them or not. And your footsteps are being ordered by the Lord: **The steps of a good man are ordered by the Lord: and he delighteth in his way** (Ps. 37:23 KJV). But even a good man will fall. **Though he fall, he shall not be utterly cast down: for the Lord upholdeth him with his hand** (Ps. 37:24 KJV).

The steps of the righteous person (the man or woman in right standing with the Lord) are ordered by the Lord. That means that if you and I are in right standing with God, we are on the right road. We are in the will of God, even if we don't know it. God is ordering our steps, even if it is through the den of lions. God will deliver us, just as He did Daniel. Even if we rebel and end up in the belly of a large fish, as Jonah did, if we will repent, God will give the fish nausea and make him spit us up on the shore — slimy and covered in seaweed, but still in the will of God.

There are many Jonahs in the Body of Christ today. Like the disobedient but repentant prophet, the Church is coming back into obedience to God. We are once again on our way.

The Desolation Is Over

In the first year of Darius son of Xerxes (a Mede by descent), who was made ruler over the Babylonian kingdom — in the first year of his reign, I, Daniel, understood from the Scriptures, according to the word of the Lord given to Jeremiah the prophet, that the desolation of Jerusalem would last seventy years.

Daniel 9:1,2

This Darius was the king of Persia during the ministry of Esther, Nehemiah, and Ezra. Again, you can see, Daniel was dealing with a world system and world and global changes.

In the first year of Darius son of Xerxes (a Mede by descent), who was made ruler over the Babylonian kingdom — in the first year of his reign I, Daniel, understood from the Scriptures.... Here is Daniel's microscopic faith. He has had telescopic faith, the distant future brought near. But it made no sense to him. In fact, it made him sick and tired. (Dan. 8:27.)

There are a lot of sick and tired prophets around today. Many pulpits in America are filled with sick and tired prophets because their visions don't make any sense, so their ministries don't make sense. They're writhing and wrestling and wearing themselves out. The enemy is attacking them in their marriages and families and finances and bodies.

...I, Daniel, understood from the Scriptures, according to the word of the Lord given to Jeremiah the

prophet, that the desolation of Jerusalem would last seventy years. Daniel is saying now that the seventy-year period has expired. This is microscopic faith.

What did the prophet Jeremiah say would happen? What does the Word of the Lord say? It says that the bondage was to be ended in seventy years. My feeling is that the equivalent of our seventy years of circumstantial captivity is up. It's time for the shackles to be loosed. It's time for the chains to fall off. It's time for revival, renewal, restoration — time for us to be conquerors.

It's time for miracles of endurance to cease and for miracles of conquest to come. The manna may stop falling upon us, but when the manna *stops* falling, the walls *start* falling.

As long as the manna was falling on the children of Israel, the walls stood around Jericho. But when God stopped the manna, when He stopped hand-feeding them, it was time for the walls of Jericho to start falling down.

"Walk across the Jordan," the Lord told them, "but get ready for the walls to come down. You can't have a pillar of cloud by day and fire by night any longer. Now you've got to grow up and walk by faith."

As long as the cloud was in front by day and fire at night, the children of Israel were in obedience. But when they crossed the Jordan, they added faith to their obedience. God is telling the Church to come into the faith realm and make our obedience spiritual and not just religious.

Daniel's Prayer

So I turned to the Lord God and pleaded with him in prayer and petition, in fasting, and in sackcloth and ashes.

Daniel 9:3

The Bible says that Daniel turned to the Lord and pleaded with Him in prayer. He began to devote himself to intercession. Prayer is another word for devotion. He began to have devotions. He went into supplication, or petition, which means asking. He entered a realm of faith in which he desired and asked of God, and then began to expect and anticipate something.

Daniel began to fast, which symbolizes and dramatizes the sincerity of prayer. Fasting is a sign of humility, yielding, obedience, acquiescence, and surrender. It represents the dying of the old flesh.

Then Daniel clothed himself in sackcloth, which signifies mourning, brokenness, repentance, contrition, or penitence. God loves those who have a broken heart and a contrite spirit. (Ps. 51:17.) Finally, he covered himself in ashes which symbolize the change or transition from death to life — renewal, restoration, revival, regeneration.

Daniel Confesses

I prayed to the Lord my God and confessed:

"O Lord, the great and awesome God, who keeps his covenant of love with all who love him and obey his commands, we have sinned and done wrong....

"Now, our God, hear the prayers and petitions of your servant. For your sake, O Lord, look with favor on your desolate sanctuary. Give ear, O God, and hear; open your eyes and see the desolation of the city that bears your Name. We do not make requests of you because we are righteous, but because of your great mercy. O Lord, listen! O Lord, forgive! O Lord, hear and act! For your sake, O my God, do not delay, because your city and your people bear your Name."

Daniel 9:4,5,17-19

Daniel's prayer was aflame with a purifier of sincere repentance. He not only prayed, he confessed his sins and the sins of his people. He interceded for them, calling upon the Lord to forgive their sins and to meet their needs, not because of their righteousness, but because of His great mercy and love. We as a Church could learn a great deal by analyzing the entire prayer of Daniel found in Verses 4 through 19.

Daniel's Revelation

In the third year of Cyrus king of Persia, a revelation was given to Daniel (who was called Belteshazzar). Its message was true and it concerned a great war. The understanding of the message came to him in a vision.

Daniel 10:1

In his long lifetime and prophetic ministry, Daniel received many visions and dreams in which he was given various revelations about the present, the past, and the future.

In the third year of Cyrus king of Persia, Daniel was given a revelation about a great war. The true translation of this verse indicates that it refers to a great conflict. There is a great conflict going on right now in the heavens. (See Eph. 3:10, 6:12.)

The understanding of the revelation came to Daniel in a vision. Sometimes Daniel received a vision and the revelation of it in a dream. Then at other times he had a dream and the interpretation came through a revelation.

Daniel Fasts

At that time I, Daniel, mourned for three weeks. I ate no choice food; no meat or wine touched my lips; and I used no lotions at all until the three weeks were over.

Daniel 10:2

Daniel was so affected by the revelation he received that he went on a restricted fast. In other words, his normal appetites and cravings changed for a season.

Daniel Receives a Vision

On the twenty-fourth day of the first month, as I was standing on the bank of the great river, the Tigris, I looked up and there before me was a man dressed in linen, with a belt of the finest gold around his waist. His body was like chrysolite, his face like

lightning, his eyes like flaming torches, his arms and
legs like the gleam of burnished bronze, and his voice
like the sound of a multitude.

Daniel 10:4-6

The word *linen* comes from the word *line* from which
we get the word *lineage*. We are of the lineage, the thread,
of Christ. You may not know it, but God is weaving and
threading a line through your life. You and I are becoming
a part of a tapestry of the glory of God.

Daniel saw a man dressed in a tapestry with a belt of
finest gold, representing (in my opinion) truth refined in
fire. His body was like chrysolite, his face like lightning and
illumination, his eyes like flaming torches, his arms and legs
like the gleam of burnished bronze.

Daniel Is Slain in the Spirit

I, Daniel, was the only one who saw the vision;
the men with me did not see it, but such terror
overwhelmed them that they fled and hid themselves.
So I was left alone, gazing at this great vision; I had
no strength left, my face turned deathly pale and I was
helpless. Then I heard him speaking, and as I listened
to him, I fell into a deep sleep, my face to the ground.

Daniel 10:7-9

Have you ever had a vision and it seemed that you were
the only one who saw it? Not even your own spouse could
see it? You probably prayed, "Lord, let somebody see this
besides me."

The men with Daniel could not see the vision, but they
could feel it, so they ran and hid themselves. If you get a
vision that only you can see, many others will be able to
feel it and will be affected by it.

I have received a vision for the destiny of my church.
As a pastor, I believe in trusting God. I'm not going to worry
about what is going to happen in the future. I've already
seen it with my spirit. If you haven't, I hope to God you
can at least feel it.

Daniel says that he was left alone. Have you ever been left alone because you are a visionary? Daniel was left gazing at this great vision of this celestial being dressed in linen. He had no strength left. His face turned deathly pale. Then he heard him speaking and as he listened to him, Daniel fell into a deep sleep, his face to the ground.

How could a person doze off when he's getting a vision like that from the Lord? Well, I think that's the only way Daniel could explain it. I don't think he was really dozing off. He was being slain in the Spirit, so he would not be impeded by his natural mind from receiving his spiritual revelation.

In the New Testament a crowd of people, perhaps two or three hundred armed with torches and clubs, came to arrest Jesus as He was praying in the Garden of Gethsemane. As Jesus got up off His knees, the place was charged with faith. He asked them, "Who are you looking for?" And they said, "Jesus of Nazareth." Jesus said, "I am He." And they were all (in my opinion) slain in the Spirit. (John 18:1-7.) Now they all fell backwards. When you fall on your face, that's humility. When you fall on your back, that's judgment. Sometimes God humbles our enemies (Goliath), and other times He outright judges them.

Being slain in the Spirit is humility, God's humility. Sometimes people have to fall because they don't always want to yield. So down they go. In the future there will be fewer people falling. I know, because I have been shown it by the Lord. God's people will learn how to stand in His presence. Sinners, doubters, and cynics will fall.

Stand Up, for Your Redemption Draweth Nigh!

A hand touched me and set me trembling on my hands and knees. He said, "Daniel, you who are highly esteemed, consider carefully the words I am about to speak to you, and stand up, for I have now been sent to you." And when he said this to me, I stood up trembling.

Daniel 10:10,11

You may be like Daniel. Perhaps you don't understand the vision. Maybe you're sick and tired and driven to your hands and knees. But even in that confused state, you're still highly esteemed of God. You don't understand why all this is happening to you, you don't even understand what's happening. You're down on your face and trembling, but the angel of the Lord is saying to you, "Stand up, for I have been sent to you."

Your Words Have Been Heard

Then he continued, "Do not be afraid, Daniel. Since the first day that you set your mind to gain understanding and to humble yourself before your God, your words were heard, and I have come in response to them."

Daniel 10:12

The angel of the Lord is saying to *you*, "When you first set your mind to gain understanding, your words were heard — and I have come in response to them."

When I first started my quest for the truth of the Lord, back before I was even in kindergarten, my words were heard. But it has taken all of these years for me to begin to receive fully what the Lord has for me. I believe the Lord is saying to this generation, "It has taken centuries of history and time and seasons to bring My plan to fulfillment, but it's coming."

Go on your way. God has a plan for you. Stay on the path. Get wrapped up. Get tied up. Get tangled up in Jesus. Don't stop praying. Don't stop asking. Stay in that mode of prayer and petition and fasting — in anything that keeps you close to the Lord — because your words are heard; your answer is on the way.

A Time Is Coming!

But the prince of the Persian kingdom resisted me twenty-one days. Then Michael, one of the chief princes, came to help me, because I was detained there with the king of Persia. Now I have come to explain

to you what will happen to your people in the future, for the vision concerns a time yet to come.
Daniel 10:13,14

The Persian kingdom represents world empires and demons, principalities which wrestle to impede or obstruct the plan of God. This Persian prince, this demonic being, resisted God's messenger for twenty-one days. Sometimes he resists angels for twenty-one years before they can bring clarity. I think that sometimes a whole generation passes with little or no light coming through.

Then Michael, one of the chief princes or archangels, one of heaven's generals, came to lend a hand. Gabriel had the message, Michael had the sword. Gabriel brings us prophesies. Michael chases devils.

When Gabriel says that he was detained there with the king of Persia, he isn't speaking in a literal sense. He means he was detained in the heavenlies by a spiritual adversary. Now he has come to explain to Daniel what will happen to his people in the future. The vision he is bringing concerns a time yet to come.

There is a message being sent to us in the Church today. It is not yet totally clear and understandable to us. We will understand it better by and by. In the meantime, we hold fast, knowing that God is at work on our behalf.

Be of good cheer, we are on our way!

15
An Altar of Prayer

Now there was a famine in the land — besides the earlier famine of Abraham's time — and Isaac went to Abimelech king of the Philistines in Gerar.

Genesis 26:1

In the days of Isaac there was a famine or recession in the land in addition to the earlier famine or depression of Abraham's time which is described in Genesis, Chapter 20.

A drought refers to a lack of rain, but a famine indicates a lack of food. There are various causes of famine. Sometimes a famine occurs because there is no rain and sometimes because there is too much rain prematurely or because the nation has been besieged by its enemies or by plagues.

Whatever the reason, there was no food in the land. The people could not eat normally. And Isaac and his family were affected like everyone else. So Isaac, Abraham's son whose name means "laughter," went to King Abimelech whose name means "father of the king."

Earlier, Abraham had gone to this same king during a famine. Abimelech was king of the Philistines. That's where we believe the word "Palestine" came from in Israel. The Philistines dominated the area in those early days, and the name Palestine may be a derivative of the word "Philistine."

Stay in the Land

The Lord appeared to Isaac and said, "Do not go down to Egypt; live in the land where I tell you to live. Stay in this land for a while, and I will be with you and will bless you. For to you and your descendants I will give all these lands and will confirm the oath I swore to your father Abraham."

Genesis 26:2,3

213

In times of famine, the tendency is always to run away, in this case to Egypt. I see going to Egypt as going backwards. Here the Lord is telling Isaac, "Do not let this famine cause you to flee to Egypt. Do not go backwards, but stay where you are and live in the land of Gerar."

Gerar is a circular region south of Jerusalem. The word really refers to a holding pattern. It means "to ruminate or cogitate, to ponder, to think." Being in Gerar is like being in between seasons.

Today in the United States, we are going through a famine or a recession. The blessing of the Lord is not evident. We don't know what to do, so the Church is kind of in a holding pattern. I believe the Lord is saying to us what He said to Isaac long ago, "Stay and live here until I tell you to move on. If you stay in this land, I will be with you and will bless you. I will give this land to you and your descendants as I have sworn."

God has a way of blessing His people and continuing His purposes even in difficult circumstances. God is going to give us something. It's just right around the corner.

Then the Lord said to Isaac, "I will confirm the oath I made to your father Abraham."

During this time of recession in our land, there are going to be confirmations of promises, covenants, and testaments. The nation must recede in some way because it will bring the country to her knees. America at large is arrogant and hostile toward God.

The United States is becoming increasingly distant from God. Secular humanism and New Age thinking have superimposed themselves over our nation's fundamental religious fervor and basic Christian heritage. So the nation is being shaken.

Most of us don't really feel the recession. When I first heard of it, I prayed that we would know about it but that no one in my congregation would ever feel it. I asked the Lord that we would never really experience the recession.

During this time of famine or want or lack or need, God is going to confirm His oaths, His covenants, His promises, and His testaments that He swore to our forefathers, including Abraham.

God's Promised Blessing

I will make your descendants as numerous as the stars in the sky and will give them all these lands, and through your offspring all nations on earth will be blessed, because Abraham obeyed me and kept my requirements, my commands, my decrees and my laws. So Isaac stayed in Gerar.

Genesis 26:4-6

The Lord is saying to us today, "I will make your descendants as numerous as the stars. You're going to keep winning souls; the Church is going to grow. And I will give to you and your offspring all of this land, this territory, and through you, all nations on earth will be blessed."

That is the Gospel in the Old Testament, as Paul says in Galatians when he notes that God ...**announced the gospel in advance to Abraham: "All nations will be blessed through you"** (Gal. 3:8). Then Paul goes on to say in verse 16: **The promises were spoken to Abraham and to his seed....meaning one person, who is Christ.**

God promised Abraham that through his seed, meaning Jesus Christ the Messiah, all nations, all ethnic groups on earth, would be blessed. In Greek one of the words translated "blessed" is *eulogetos,* from which we get the word "eulogy," meaning high praise, as when we eulogize someone who has died.

The Lord is saying to us, "If you will stay where you are, as Isaac did, then through your seed, all nations will have a chance to be eulogized by Me." God will eulogize us Christians. Our works will praise us into the gates, and there the Father will eulogize us.

215

Hold Fast to Your Commitment

When the men of that place asked him about his wife, he said, "She is my sister," because he was afraid to say, "She is my wife." He thought, "The men of this place might kill me on account of Rebekah, because she is beautiful."

Genesis 26:7

The same thing had happened to Isaac's father in Chapter 20. These same people had asked about Abraham's wife. He, too, had said, "She is my sister." (v. 2.)

Isaac lied. His father, Abraham, half lied, because Sarah was his half-sister and his wife. But the point is that for some reason both of these men were afraid.

During this time of recession, the world is going to say to us believers, "Is this your sibling or your love?" In other words, "Is this just a casual independent relationship you have with another person, or is this your commitment?"

When the men of this place asked Isaac about his wife — that is, who he was married to, what he was committed to — he denied his relationship. He claimed that he and Rebekah were not husband and wife but brother and sister. He did so because he was afraid to say, "She is my true love and life's commitment."

Some folks, during this recession, are going to be afraid to tell the world that they truly love and are fully committed to Jesus Christ, that they're really married to the Gospel, that they have made a life commitment and are totally devoted to their call. Like Abraham and Isaac, they're going to waffle a little bit.

Isaac thought, "The men of this place might kill me on the account of Rebekah because she's so beautiful." In the same way, some are going to become jealous of the beauty of our union with Christ. But we must not back away from our commitment.

Our relationship is going to look so beautiful during this recession. Our commitment, our devotion to each other and to our Lord, is going to be so attractive that others are going to want to take it from us.

Stay With God's Plan

When Isaac had been there a long time, Abimelech king of the Philistines looked down from a window and saw Isaac caressing his wife Rebekah. So Abimelech summoned Isaac and said, "She is really your wife! Why did you say, 'She is my sister'?"

Isaac answered him, "Because I thought I might lose my life on account of her."

Genesis 26:8,9

Isaac had been there a long time. Sometimes the recession lasts.

Right now we are in a holding pattern, waiting for further instructions. God's plan is in no way hindered and cannot be thwarted by recession. He has assured us, "I'm going to keep My covenants, My promises. Everything is going to proceed right on schedule. The world will have recession or famine, but My plans will not be affected. You just stay with the flow." God has a plan that we don't know about.

Abimelech, king of the Philistines, looked down from a window and saw Isaac caressing his wife whom he had denied. In the same way, some believers will say, "I'm not really committed," but in secret they'll be caressing their mates. They will still be praying, reading the Bible, and going to church because they can't leave God. And the world is going to be watching them.

Abimelech summoned Isaac and said to him, "This woman is really your wife! Why did you say that she's your sister? Why did you say that she's just an independent sibling or an equal? Why didn't you tell me you're in love with this woman? Why didn't you acknowledge that you had a commitment? Why are you so willing to compromise?"

This king wasn't eager to compromise. Earlier he had seen the same thing happen with Isaac's father. King Abimelech recalled that when he took Abraham's wife to himself, God appeared to him in a dream and judged him. And he almost died. (Gen. 20.) So now he is very reverent because he has no desire to offend God again by interfering with His chosen vessels.

Do Not Molest God's Servants

Then Abimelech said, "What is this you have done to us? One of the men might well have slept with your wife, and you would have brought guilt upon us."

So Abimelech gave orders to all the people: "Anyone who molests this man or his wife shall surely be put to death."

Genesis 26:10,11

The world has laughed at what has been happening recently to some well-known ministers and televangelists.

It is nobody's responsibility to put down a man of God but God Himself. God lifts people up and He can put them down. It's best for us to keep our hands off them. That doesn't mean that we say everything they say, do everything they do, and support their ministries. But we must not denounce them, judge them, or blaspheme against them.

God knows what He's doing. He called these people and raised them up. He can bring them down when He wants to. If we take it on ourselves to deal with them, we might come under His retroactive judgment.

Throughout biblical history when God's people failed or backslid, He allowed others to overcome them. And after His people had been chastened, then the Lord turned against their invaders and judged them.

I am prophesying that in the days ahead, it will become clear that God judges those who judge His own. In the hard times that America is about to go through, many will reconsider whether or not they should pass judgment on the Church.

Planting and Reaping in Famine

Isaac planted crops in that land and the same year reaped a hundredfold, because the Lord blessed him. The man became rich, and his wealth continued to grow until he became very wealthy.

Genesis 26:12,13

Don't be afraid of all this talk about recession and depression. Even if it comes, it will never affect us, not when we're in the divine will of God.

The warning signals are already being sent out. It is being predicted that by 1993 prices will go sky high. Property values are supposed to be out of reach in a matter of months. The market is soft in most of the United States. It's a buyer's market, not a seller's. It's not a time to sell, it's a time to buy — if you have the money, which many people don't.

In the midst of hard times, Isaac planted crops. In famine he gave. He sowed his seed even during recession.

Our church carried on a $1.1 million renovation of our building right in the middle of the religious scandals when the whole Church was shaking. All of our people gave anyway, and today everything we did is paid for. I had thought that by now things would be much better. But here we are in a so-called recession.

The Lord said to me, "You've got to have your multi-purpose center, your children's work. So what are you going to do?" And He showed me that Isaac planted crops in that land, right in that holding pattern, right in Gerar. Right while he cogitated and pondered. Right while he was wondering, "God, where do I go from here? I'm in a cycle, a holding pattern. I can't go forward, and I can't go backwards. What shall I do?"

The Lord's answer to Isaac was, "Give. Plant right there in that land." **...and the same year reaped a hundredfold, because the Lord blessed him** (v. 12).

You and I can plant our seed and reap a hundredfold even during famine, because the Lord will bless us. All we have to do is stay where God places us. This is no time to go down to Egypt, no time to backslide, no time to be afraid, no time to hold back.

"Plant," says the Lord. "Sow your seed in the land where you are, and I'll bless you as long as you're in obedience."

But remember the Lord your God, for it is he who gives you the ability to produce wealth, and so confirms his covenant, which he swore to your forefathers, as it is today (Deut. 8:18). God's covenant will not be thwarted.

God has a covenant that is not yet completely fulfilled. We are a part of that covenant, that promise. Regardless of what happens to the world around us, God's covenant with us will continue to be fulfilled.

I am part of a covenant, part of the promise, and part of God's fulfillment. Therefore I will not change, even though I'm in a holding pattern. I can't land, and I can't take off. The traffic is backed up. So I'm going to plant where I'm holding. I'm going to sow what I'm holding. And God is going to give me a hundredfold return — this year. **Isaac planted crops in that land and *the same year* reaped a hundredfold, because the Lord blessed him** (v. 12).

Underline this next part: **The man became *rich*...** This took place during a famine, during a recession. Isaac wasn't rich when he got to Gerar, but because he stayed in the land and was obedient to the Lord, God prospered him greatly **...and his wealth continued to grow until he became very wealthy** (v. 13). If we are obedient to the Lord, we, too, will become rich and our wealth will continue to grow until we become very wealthy.

In my church, we haven't made a doctrine of the prosperity message. We hardly ever preach it. But right now, because people are afraid of recession, I feel I need to bring this word from the Lord.

I believe God is going to make millionaires out of all of us, which means we're going to have more money to give to God's work. I expect that in my lifetime our annual church budget will be hundreds of millions of dollars which we will invest into the Gospel. We're going to be planting the Word of God all over the world.

I felt the faith to go out and buy sixty acres of property to use to bring in and train inner-city troubled teens. Our plan is get them out of the asphalt jungles and show them a better way, and then prepare them to go right into school, either Rhema Bible Training Center or Oral Roberts University. One reason I want to do this is because I don't feel like it's right for me to go into the inner city, preach the Gospel, take money out, and never give anything back to the people. I know God will give us more so we can invest it in helping others.

The Church must make the difference. We can't wait for the government to do it. Isaac planted crops and reaped a hundredfold return in famine. We intend to do the same thing. We plan to plant our seed during the recession, believing that we will reap a hundredfold return the same year. We believe that, like Isaac, we will become rich, and that our wealth will grow until we become very wealthy.

The Envy of the World

He had so many flocks and herds and servants that the Philistines envied him.
Genesis 26:14

The world is going to become envious of us Christians because of our prosperity in the midst of recession. While banks and financial institutions are going under and hundred-million-dollar companies are folding, God's people are going to be increasing and expanding. Because we are obedient to the Lord, we are going to be blessed of Him to do what we're supposed to do. And the world will be envious of us.

Plugging Up the Wells

So all the wells that his father's servants had dug in the time of his father Abraham, the Philistines stopped up, filling them with earth.

Genesis 26:15

These wells had been dug to find water during time of drought. They are symbolic. Digging deep into the depths of the earth represents digging deep into the depths of God and being refreshed.

The world hates our water. They hate our lifestyle, our spirit. They are jealous of our prosperity. They want to plug up our wells, to stop our joy, to alter our lifestyle, to hinder our flow, and to break our anointing — because this is an antichrist spirit.

Remember, the word *Christ* or *Messiah* means "the anointed one." To be anointed is to have something like oil rubbed or smeared on you. When we were anointed, God rubbed and smeared Himself on us. We are anointed with Christ. The spirit of this world is an antichrist, anti-anointing spirit.

Just as blood usually represents life, water generally represents Spirit. So God is saying to us in this passage, "When you dig the wells, you will strike water, the Spirit of life."

Remember, Jesus said, "If you believe on Me, as the Scriptures have said, out of your innermost being will flow rivers of living water." (John 7:38.) In John 4:14 He said, **"...whoever drinks the water I give him will never thirst. Indeed, the water I give him will become a spring of water welling up to eternal life."**

Everywhere we go, we are going to be giving forth fountains of living water. Folks are going to be going through the famine thirsty, and here comes one of God's Holy Ghost-filled people. Suddenly a fountain of life-giving Spirit will burst forth flowing in every direction.

Others are going to want to drink from that fountain, but they're going to be so jealous and envious they will try to stop the flow. They will do anything in their power to kill the Spirit, to plug up the wells. They will start filling them up with earth, with dust, with dirt. Earth or dust or dirt represent the flesh. The world will try to plug up our wells with flesh just as they are trying to stop the television evangelists by using the flesh. They are going to try to plug up our churches, our ministries, our outreaches. We're not going to let them do that.

Move On!

Then Abimelech said to Isaac, "Move away from us; you have become too powerful for us."

Genesis 26:16

"Get out of here," said the king to Isaac. "You're too powerful, too rich, too influential. Pack up your belongings and clear out of our land."

The Wells Reopened

So Isaac moved from there and encamped in the Valley of Gerar and settled there. Isaac reopened the wells that had been dug in the time of his father Abraham, which the Philistines had stopped up after Abraham died, and he gave them the same names his father had given them.

Genesis 26:17,18

Isaac did as the king requested and moved away to the Valley of Gerar where he reopened his father's wells.

The world has plugged up many of our wells, the old wells of the Spirit, of holiness, of Pentecost, the old wells of healing, miracles, and deliverance. But we're going to reopen them, every one of them. The Spirit is going to flow freely and freshly. Even though the world gets upset with us, we're just going to keep on digging.

When Isaac reopened the wells, he gave them the same names, the same authorization, that his father Abraham had given them. He honored his father by doing that. The wells represent the sons of the next generation. Like Isaac, we are going to reopen the wells that our forefathers dug, and we're not going to try to change their names. We're going to give them the same authorization.

Keep Digging!

Isaac's servants dug in the valley and discovered a well of fresh water there. But the herdsmen of Gerar quarreled with Isaac's herdsmen and said, "The water is ours!" So he named the well Esek ("dispute"), because they disputed with him. Then they dug another well, but they quarreled over that one also; so he named it Sitnah ("opposition"). He moved on from there and dug another well, and no one quarreled over it. He named it Rehoboth ("room"), saying, "Now the Lord has given us room and we will flourish in the land."

Genesis 26:19-22

We've got to keep digging, even if we are driven away. If we are ordered to leave town, we will move into the valley, but we will keep on digging until we discover a well of fresh water.

Even when we are chased away, we're going to find more fresh water in the valley than we found where we were. Anything the world does to us is going to boomerang on them. If they try to shut us down, we're going to keep on digging. If they slander us, we're going to keep on digging. If they tell lies about us, we're going to keep on digging. If they ridicule us, we're going to keep on digging. And the deeper we dig, the fresher the water will be.

Some of the wells we dig are going to cause dispute or strife. Folks are going to dispute us, but we must keep on digging because they disputed Isaac in his day. But when that happened, he just dug another well.

When some folks encounter strife, they quit digging. They quit praying and working and worshipping because it makes them unpopular. It brings criticism and false accusation upon them. We must not be deterred by the opinions or actions of others.

When the second well that Isaac dug caused strife, he named it Sitnah, which means opposition, hostility, or accusation. So he just moved away and dug someplace else. When we dig our wells, there may be strife, opposition, hostility, or accusation. We, too, must move on and dig elsewhere.

Finally, Isaac dug a new well and no one quarreled with him over it, so he named it Rehoboth. The word *Rehoboth* means "room, space, expanse." If Isaac had given up after digging the first two wells which caused strife, opposition, hostility, and accusation, he would never have gotten to the place where God could make room for him. Room for growth, blessings, dreams, visions, aspirations, ambitions.

The same is true for us today.

Keep digging until you find enough space to live. Keep digging until you find enough space to give. Keep digging until fresh water comes, until the devil has to get back out of the way. Dig, dig, dig.

In our church we have kept digging until the Lord has given us room. He has given us growth. We are about to flourish — right now. Right in the midst of recession, right in the midst of famine, we are about to prosper and grow in the Lord.

God's Promised Increase

From there he went up to Beersheba. That night the Lord appeared to him and said, "I am the God of your father Abraham. Do not be afraid, for I am with you; I will bless you and will increase the number of your descendants for the sake of my servant Abraham."

Genesis 26:23,24

The name *Beersheba* means either "well of the oath" or "well of seven."[1] But that wasn't its name when Isaac first arrived there.

While he was in that place, the Lord appeared to him and promised to be with him, to bless him, and to increase the number of his descendants for the sake of his father, Abraham.

What God was saying to Isaac is, "I am going to increase the number of your offspring, the number of the things you produce through the Spirit. I'm going to increase you in fruits, in faith, in gifts.

God is making that same promise to us today. He is going to increase us in descendants, in offspring, in fruits, in faith, and in gifts. Here's a key to that promise.

Call on the Lord

Isaac built an altar there and called on the name of the Lord. There he pitched his tent, and there his servants dug a well.

Genesis 26:25

Wherever you are, build an altar, call on the Lord, establish residence with Him, and dig your well.

In this verse, the phrase "built an altar" means that Isaac participated in sacrificial giving. In Hebrew the word translated *altar* is derived from a root word meaning "slaughter." To sacrifice is to slaughter, to give up life. To us an altar is a place to pray, but to the ancient Jews an altar was a place of sacrifice, a place to give.

Before we come to the altar of the Lord to pray, we must first bring an offering. We've got to give before we pray, not pray before we give.

---

[1]Footnote to Genesis 26:33, *The Holy Bible: New International Version*, copyright © 1973, 1978, 1984 by the International Bible Society. Used by permission of Zondervan Bible Publishers.

So, wherever you are, build an altar. Make a sacrifice of yourself. Then call on the name of the Lord.

Isaac's pitching his tent is representative of tabernacling in God's presence. Establish residence, abide in the Lord, and then start digging for the wells of the Spirit to come forth.

Living in Beersheba

Meanwhile, Abimelech had come to him from Gerar, with Ahuzzath his personal adviser and Phicol the commander of his forces. Isaac asked them, "Why have you come to me, since you were hostile to me and sent me away?"

They answered, "We saw clearly that the Lord was with you; so we said, 'There ought to be a sworn agreement between us' — between us and you. Let us make a treaty with you that you will do us no harm, just as we did not molest you but always treated you well and sent you away in peace. And now you are blessed by the Lord."

Isaac then made a feast for them, and they ate and drank. Early the next morning the men swore an oath to each other. Then Isaac sent them on their way, and they left him in peace.

That day Isaac's servants came and told him about the well they had dug. They said, "We've found water!" He called it Shibah ("oath" or "seven"), and to this day the name of the town has been Beersheba ("well of the oath" or "well of seven").

Genesis 26:26-33

One day there is going to be a peace treaty between the government, the military, and the Church. They will come to us and say, "Let us make a treaty with you so that you will do us no harm."

It may not be at this particular time, but on down through the years as we continue in faith and obedience, God is going to begin to open to us doors of prosperity and power and peace. And everyone will see that we are blessed by the Lord.

These same men who had earlier rejected Isaac and sent him away came to him seeking a non-aggression pact with him. The very day these men left in peace, Isaac's servants came to him about the well they had dug. They said to him, "We have found water!"

Isaac named that final well Shebah. The Hebrew word *shebah* means "seven" or "oath." Seven is the number of commitment, devotion, oath.

Because we are committed to the Lord, devoted to Him, because we have an oath, an agreement, a covenant with Him, everywhere we go we will find water. We will always be living in Beersheba!

OTHER BOOKS
BY CARLTON PEARSON

Birth of a Vision

Breaking the Curse

Hope — In Spite of the Circumstances

Armed for Battle

Crisis at the Crossroads

**Available from your local bookstore,
or from:**

Harrison House
P. O. Box 35035
Tulsa, OK 74153

Carlton Pearson pastors one of the fastest-growing churches in Tulsa, Oklahoma — Higher Dimensions. Started in 1981 as a storefront gathering of 75 people, today it is a multi-faceted ministry of more than 3,000 people.

The congregation of Higher Dimensions is composed of many ages, races and cultures. One newspaper called it "a sociologist's fantasy, a compilation of people from every socio-economic class . . . a racial melting pot." Pastor Pearson prefers to call it "a stew." In a stew each ingredient stays as it is, but together they begin to take on the "flavor" of one another. He places a high priority on family and country, reflected in his first television special, entitled: "America, We Love You."

Pastor Pearson serves on the board of regents at Oral Roberts University, as well as on the boards of several Christian missionary organizations. He has authored a variety of books and booklets carrying the message of deliverance: that Jesus Christ came to forgive the sins of all men and save their souls.

To contact Carlton Pearson, write:
P. O. Box 700007
Tulsa, OK 74170

*Please include your prayer requests
and comments when you write.*